WA 1384396 6

POLICY AND PRACTICE IN HEALT

NUMBER TWO

D1580861

Direct Payments and
Personalisation of Care

POLICY AND PRACTICE IN HEALTH AND SOCIAL CARE

POLICY AND PRACTICE IN HEALTH AND SOCIAL CARE

SERIES EDITORS

JOYCE CAVAYE and ALISON PETCH

Direct Payments and Personalisation of Care

edited by

Charlotte Pearson

Lecturer in Public Policy
Department of Urban Studies
The University of Glasgow

DUNEDIN ACADEMIC PRESS

EDINBURGH

Published by
Dunedin Academic Press Ltd
Hudson House
8 Albany Street
Edinburgh EH1 3QB
Scotland

ISBN 10: 1 903765 62 5
ISBN 13: 978-1903-765-61-6
ISSN 1750-1407

© 2006 Dunedin Academic Press

*The right of Charlotte Pearson and the contibutors to be identified as
the authors of this work has been asserted by her in accordance with
sections 77 and 78 of the Copyright, Designs and Patents Act 1988*

British Library Cataloguing in Publication data
A catalogue record for this book is available from the British Library

Typeset by Makar Publishing Production
Printed and bound in Great Britain by Cromwell Press

Contents

Series Editors Introduction

Direct Payments are widely regarded as making a key contribution to the independence, well being and quality of life of people with disabilities. When introduced almost a decade ago they were seen as a victory for the rights of disabled people. Heralded as the means to empower service users, direct payments were intended to allow them control and choice over the services they used to meet their needs.

Since the initial implementation of direct payments there have been a number of key changes to the policy framework. While these changes have taken place across the UK, there has been a different pattern in take-up and policy development in Scotland where attempts have been made to integrate direct payments into a wider policy agenda focused on the personalisation of care. Implementing direct payments requires an operational shift in approach to the concepts of risk and control. This presents a challenge to the traditional culture of service provision and delivery and has resulted in a degree of resistance amongst practitioners.

This book, edited by Charlotte Pearson, provides a clear account of the development of direct payments and explores some of the conceptual as well as political debates about their role, purpose and implementation. Drawing on empirical research, the authors use a case study approach to critically assess the experiences and attitudes of service users and local authorities towards Direct Payments. This book moves behind the policy rhetoric to explore some of the tensions in the implementation of the user-led model of direct payments supported by the Scottish Executive. Implementing direct payments is a challenge for policy-makers and practitioners but this book provides a real sense of possibilities for the future.

Dr Joyce Cavaye
Faculty of Health and Social Care,
The Open University in Scotland,
Edinburgh

Professor Alison Petch
Director, Research in Practice for
Adults, *The Dartington Hall Trust,*
Totnes, Devon, U.K

Glossary of Abbreviations

BCODP   British Council of Disabled People
CIL   Centre for Independent Living
DIG   Disablement Income Group
DLA   Disability Living Allowance
DoH   Department of Health
DPS   Direct Payments Scotland
DRC   Disability Rights Commission
DSS   Department of Social Security
ESRC   Economic and Social Research Council
GCIL   Glasgow Centre for Independent Living
HSS   health and social service trust(s) (in Northern Ireland)
ILCDP   *Improving the Life Chances of Disabled People*
ILF   Independent Living Fund
SPAEN   Scottish Personal Assistants Employers Network

CHAPTER 1

Introduction:
The Development of Direct Payments in Scotland

Charlotte Pearson and Sheila Riddell

This chapter offers an introduction to the themes and data which will be explored throughout this book. A decade after the implementation of the Community Care (Direct Payments) Act in 1997, this book provides an overview of the key issues that have impacted on implementation in Scotland.

What are direct payments and why are they important?

The Community Care (Direct Payments) Act 1996 gave local authorities across Britain (and health and social service trusts (HSS) in Northern Ireland), the powers to make cash payments to disabled people. Initially this was restricted to people under the age of 65 with physical and sensory impairments, learning difficulties and mental health problems, but was later amended to include older people, 16- and 17-year-olds, parents of disabled children and, in England, Wales and Northern Ireland only, carers.

Legislation established eligibility for a direct payment through local community care procedures, thereby enabling access through the same assessment system as directly provided social services. This has distinguished policy from other examples of direct payments for disabled people such as the Independent Living Fund (ILF), which is paid through central government funding to a designated charity, and social security payments such as the Disability Living Allowance (DLA). Likewise, the payment of monies directly to the service user from the local authority, rather than through a third party, differentiates policy from earlier cash payment schemes. These are explored in more detail later in this chapter.

Direct payments give users control over money spent on meeting their community care needs rather than receiving services arranged for them by their local authority. They have therefore become an important social policy through their capacity to empower service users through the receipt of a cash sum funded by the state to buy in a specific service. Indeed as commentary throughout the book details, the issue of control has been a key focus for the disability movement in their campaign to secure direct payments on the statute book. Likewise, the locus of control of direct payments has also emerged as an underlying theme for successive Conservative and New Labour Governments, as they have sought to integrate direct payments into a wider agenda focused on the personalisation of care.

Structure of the book

This book draws on a range of research produced over this period, including new data from a two-year UK-wide study of direct payments funded by the Economic and Social Research Council (ESRC)[1] and conducted by the authors (Pearson, Riddell and Williams) together with colleagues from the University of Leeds (Professor Colin Barnes, Debbie Jolly, Dr Geof Mercer and Dr Mark Priestley) from January 2005 to June 2006. The research presented in this book focuses primarily on the Scottish aspect of the study, but makes some comparisons with the wider UK context. Full details of the study and methodologies used are given in appendix 1.

Drawing on Scottish and wider UK literature, this chapter explores some of the tensions within direct payments policy which have emerged over the past decade. We begin by looking at the role of indirect payments in Scotland, funded through central government programmes such as the Independent Living Fund and the Independent Living Transfer. Discussion then moves to look at the emergence of formal legislation for direct payments under the Conservative Government led by John Major. Although initially hostile to direct payments, the Conservative administration eventually decided that these might contribute to the wider marketisation of social care agenda, a theme which is developed further in this book.

In chapter 2, Pearson describes the micro-politics and cultures of welfare operating in two Scottish local authorities, the first broadly supportive of the development of direct payments, the second reflecting considerable resistance. In chapter 3, the focus shifts to an examination of the role of support organisations, often seen as central to the success of direct payments. However, as Pearson shows, there have been significant differences in the allocation of funding for support and the types of structure in place across the UK and in Scotland. The drive to promote support organisations and the preferred user-led model north of the border was initially promoted by Direct Payments Scotland (DPS) (DPS, 2002) and has been supported in guidance by the Scottish Executive (Scottish Executive, 2003a). To date, there are 25 support organisations up and running in the 32 local authorities. The situation in Scotland contrasts with that in England where there appears to be declining enthusiasm for user-led support organisations (Barnes and Mercer, 2006). Issues around control and funding of support organisations therefore remain prominent.

In chapter 4, Riddell's discussion considers how direct payments have been used as part of a wider marketisation of care in Scotland and throughout the UK. Through a series of telephone interviews with leading direct payments personnel across local authorities in Scotland, chapter 4 explores the impact of the marketisation agenda in more detail. Drawing on analysis from the telephone interviews with local authority personnel and findings from the case studies (outlined in chapter 2), the commentary underlines how the struggle between market and independent living discourses have been played out in local areas.

Given the importance of disabled people's activism in securing direct payments on the statute book, the experiences and opinions of users are central to gauging the success or failure of policy. In chapter 5, Williams sets out the main issues as described by users in focus groups and interviews. As she explains, whilst the ethos and focus of direct payments remains popular and has signified an important shift towards the realisation of independent living goals, local interpretations and the frameworks put in place through this clearly impact on user experiences of direct payments.

Chapter 6 concludes by exploring the future possibilities for direct payments in Scotland, focusing on some of the more recent policy developments informed by the 'personalisation of care' agenda and promoted through the various UK jurisdictions.

A decade of direct payments: policy development issues in Scotland

Direct payments were implemented in England, Wales and Scotland in April 1997 through provisions set out in the 1996 Community Care (Direct Payments) Act. The original policy framework enabled local authorities to make cash payments to service users with physical and sensory impairments, learning difficulties and mental health problems. At this stage, access was restricted to people under the age of 65, although in June 2000, it was extended to older people (Scottish Executive, 2000a), followed by 16- and 17-year-olds, and parents of disabled children. Carers were also included in England, Wales and Northern Ireland, but not in Scotland. A key feature of the original legislation was its position as enabling legislation. This gave local authorities, and health and social service trusts in Northern Ireland, the option whether to allocate direct payments or maintain existing modes of service provision. This initiated an uneven development of direct payments across the UK (see Riddell et al., 2005), with particularly poor uptake in Scotland.

Changes set out in the Community Care and Health (Scotland) Act 2002 and related legislation elsewhere in the UK sought to challenge this pattern by setting in place a mandatory duty on all local authorities to offer direct payments to all eligible people requesting one. In light of these recent changes, one of the key aims of this book is to explore their impact across Scotland.

However, before doing this, attention is shifted to mapping the background to policy development in Scotland. This begins by exploring the origins of direct payments through the role of disability activism and local champions of policy within key local authorities. The impact of these alliances is then examined in the light of implementation of the 1996 Community Care (Direct Payments) Act. This will initiate a more in-depth look throughout the book at the tensions that have emerged in the first decade of policy implementation.

Early payment patterns: exploring the role of disability activism in Scotland

Prior to implementation of the 1996 Act, confusion surrounded the legality of direct payments across the UK (Pearson, 2006). In England and Wales, the 1948 Social Security Act stipulated that only services and not payments could be made by local authorities, but the position differed slightly in Scotland. Indeed, provisions set out in section 12 of the Social Work (Scotland) Act 1968 meant cash payments could be made available by local authorities 'in exceptional circumstances constituting an emergency' (see Roll, 1996). However, the impact of this ruling was limited, with minimal knowledge of this guidance among local authority practitioners (Pearson, 2000) and evidence of only one area making payments through this route (Witcher et al., 2000).

Throughout the 1980s and 1990s, indirect payments administered through third parties, such as voluntary sector organisations or independent local trusts, were used in some areas to overcome the broader UK-wide restriction to policy. Central to these changes were the roles of small groups of disabled people demanding a more flexible alternative to rigid and paternalistic modes of service provision offered to them by local authorities. Most of this activism occurred in England, where disabled people in areas such as Hampshire, Essex, Norfolk and Derbyshire initiated these challenges. In Scotland, although developments were more limited, pockets of activism also emerged. These were led mainly from the former Lothian region, where the local authorities permitted three initial payments to be made under the provisions of the 1968 Act. Whilst the local authority enabled the payments to go ahead, problems arose when, in 1995, the then Department of Social Security (DSS) became alerted to this practice and suspended the Income Support payments of those involved. This resulted from a circular issued by the Department of Health, which stated that all forms of direct payments made through local authorities were illegal. Consequently a challenge to the case in Lothian was made and won by the local authority, but the case had raised the profile of cash payments, thereby instigating the need for a formal legislative path to be developed.

Other examples of indirect payments in Scotland also emerged at this time in the light of wider policy shifts from central government (Pearson, 2006). Notably in the former Strathclyde region, monies paid from the Independent Living Transfer (ILT) helped establish an alternative model of indirect payments (see Kestenbaum, 1995). ILT funds were made available to local authorities as community care was being rolled out to allow them to develop 'independent living' services for disabled people in the area. Unlike the payments being made in response to the demands of disabled people in key local authorities, funding for this approach came from central government. This emerged from wider changes amidst a reorganisation of social security for disabled people and the development of community care policy from the late 1980s (Glendinning, 1992) by the then Conservative Government. Part of this strategy also included the launch of the Independent Living Fund (ILF), which allowed another route to indirect payments to emerge. The ILF was set up in co-operation with the Disablement Incomes Group (DIG) – a national campaigning organisation of disabled people – to compensate for the loss of additional domestic payments made to disabled people removed by the social security reforms. In the light of these changes, concerns had been raised (Glendinning, 1992) that some disabled people would be forced to enter residential care – an outcome that clearly conflicted with the push towards 'care in the community' being promoted at the time. The launch of the ILF was initially seen as a temporary measure to cover gaps in support for disabled people prior to the implementation of community care in April 1993. However, its importance was perhaps more symbolic, in that it represented the first large-scale opportunity for disabled people in the UK to use cash for personal assistance, rather than relying on services provided by local authorities or families (Zarb and Nadash, 1994).

The main part of the ILT – the social security element – was the difference between what would have been paid by the DSS to people entering residential and nursing homes and what was then to be paid by way of the normal Income Support and Residential Allowance (Kestenbaum, 1992). As Kestenbaum notes, the ILT was therefore of great importance to disabled people because it was clearly designated for 'independent living' services. It was not, however, ring-fenced and in many local authorities was simply swallowed up into other services. Strathclyde's response to the ILT was therefore important as it represented one of the few local authorities in the UK which used ILT funds for its intended purpose – to develop a distinct independent living strategy. From 1995 this was used to establish the Centre for Independent Living (CIL) as well as providing funding for six personal assistant advisers (employed through the Social Work Department) and developing an indirect payments scheme. Whilst this proved very popular with local disabled people, its position as a separate service option, rather than part of mainstream disability services, restricted access to new users and has made it susceptible to cuts since the outset.

The ILF and ILT therefore represented alternative routes to develop personal assistance schemes prior to formal adoption of direct payments. Despite initial concerns by a number of disability groups over the replacement of legal entitlements to benefits with discretionary awards from a charity (Wood, 1991), implementation proved to be remarkably successful, bringing considerable benefits for disabled people (Kestenbaum, 1992), and demand greatly exceeded government projections. Given that funding for the ILF was awarded from central government, many other local authorities who were reluctant to embrace indirect payments also welcomed the scheme.

The ILF was only originally intended to be a temporary measure. However, its popularity because of increased choice, control and flexibility for users led to a reconsideration of plans. This saw the fund replaced with two – albeit more restrictive – new charitable trusts. Existing users continued to receive payments through the Independent Living (Extension) Fund, and the Independent Living Fund 1993 (ILF '93) was run alongside services provided or purchased by local authorities.

Mapping the market: direct payments and the marketisation of care

As indicated so far, implementation of the 1996 Act represented a significant victory for the disability movement. Whilst the then Conservative Government initiated the legislative path, there were considerable reservations as to the merits of direct payments throughout much of the early 1990s. These centred largely around issues of cost efficiency, whereby the allocation of cash rather than services raised concerns as to the accountability of government monies (House of Lords debate, 18 June 1990, cited in Roll, 1996). However, after publication of research into personal assistance schemes carried out for the British Council of Disabled People (BCODP) (Zarb and Nadash, 1994), a shift in government opinion emerged. Significantly, the research showed direct payments to be around 40% cheaper than directly provided services. For an administration committed to an agenda of cost savings and efficiency, this proved to be a powerful base for the BCODP to challenge the government's position. Indeed, a week after publication it was announced that legislation for direct payments would emerge on the statute book (Pearson, 2000).

The policy framework for direct payments therefore developed through both independent living (or social justice) and market discourses (Pearson, 2000). On the one hand, campaigning from the disability movement at both national and local levels was important in establishing momentum for change. However, as noted, the appeal for the Conservative Government rested in its positioning of direct payments as part of a wider 'marketisation of care', established initially through the 1990 Community Care Act. This framed direct payments as an instrument for accessing choice and diversity in service provision through the development of 'local care markets'. New Labour have subsequently utilised this approach as the basis of their broader modernisation programme in social care with its increasing focus on 'personalising' services (see, for example, Leadbeater, 2004). This will be returned to shortly.

Initial take-up: 1997–2000

As detailed elsewhere (see Pearson, 2004a, 2006), the early years of policy implementation in Scotland were characterised by a very low take-up. This was confirmed in the first major study of direct payments, carried out by Witcher et al. (2000). This research, commissioned by the Scottish Executive, underlined the limited availability of direct payments, with only 13 out of the 32 local authorities adopting fully operational or pilot schemes and a total of 143 users. By contrast, around the same time individual English authorities such as Hampshire had around 400 users. Findings from Witcher et al.'s research also highlighted an imbalance between impairment groups, with nearly 90% uptake for people with physical and sensory impairments, and only marginal use for people with learning difficulties. At this time, there were no users with reported mental health problems and the number of users from black and minority ethnic communities was also disproportionately poor.

Policy change since 2000: the profile of direct payments users

Although take-up of direct payments in Scotland and the rest of the UK (see Riddell et al., 2005) was especially poor during the initial period of implementation, the Scottish Executive – like the rest of the UK administrations – underlined its commitment to policy through a series of legislative changes. In Scotland, this focused on extending policy to a more diverse user population and presenting changes as part of the modernising agenda for social care and social inclusion (Scottish Executive, 2003a).

The early shift in June 2000 to grant people over the age of 65 access to a direct payment was followed up by a more comprehensive set of reforms outlined in the Community Care and Health (Scotland) Act 2002. Central to these changes was the enforcement of a mandatory duty placed on all local authorities to offer direct payments to all eligible groups from June 2003. Although the same shift was made across the UK, outside England the implications of the move looked to be more strongly felt because of the low initial take-up (Pearson, 2006 and chapter 4). The 2002 Act also allowed parents of disabled children to receive payments but did not include access to carers – a move that differed from change elsewhere in the UK.

As well as excluding carers from the Act, it was stipulated at this time that all people assessed as having 'community care needs' would be eligible for a direct payment. This provision covered people who are frail, receiving rehabilitation after an accident or operation, fleeing domestic violence, are a refugee, homeless or recovering from drug or alcohol dependency. The change was initially planned for April 2004 but, amid concerns that local authorities and support organisations would be unable to cope with new user groups (Pearson, 2004b), the proposal was withdrawn. However, this intended shift perhaps underlines the Executive's long-term interest in the direct payments model across social care services.

By March 2005, the number of people in receipt of direct payments had reached 1,438 (see Figure 1.1), representing a seven-fold increase on the number of users in 2001. However, despite this rapid increase, uptake remains slow and access to payments between user groups varies considerably. As demonstrated by Figure 1.2, people with physical disabilities, particularly in the under-65 age group, continue to receive the majority of payments.

There has also been a marked increase in the amount of money spent by local authorities on direct payments (see Figure 1.3). Again, people with physical disabilities capture the lion's share of resource.

There are major discrepancies in the use of direct payments by local authorities (see Figure 1.4), with Fife having the largest number of users, followed by the City of Edinburgh, which accounts for half of all expenditure in Scotland. When these figures are presented as a proportion of the population, the use of direct payments by different local authorities appears slightly different, with small rural authorities exceeding large urban authorities (see Figure 1.5).

Compared with England, Scotland makes less use of direct payments, although it has a higher proportion of users than Northern Ireland and Wales. Table 1.1 shows the use of direct payments calculated as a proportion of the population with a limiting long-term illness or disability.

Table 1.1 Direct payment users in each country/province of the UK between 2000/01 and 2003: number and rate per thousand people with LTID

Country/ province	Population (millions)	% LTID[1]	Number of direct payment users and rate per thousand people with LTID					
			2000/01		2002/03		2003	
England	50	18	4,900	(0.54)	6,300	(0.7)	9,700	(1.0)
Scotland	5	20	207	(0.20)	392	(0.4)	571	(0.57)
Wales[2]	3	23	*	*	185	(0.26)	*	*
Northern Ireland	1.5	23	33	(0.09)	49	(0.14)	128	(0.37)

[1] This column shows the percentage of the population who reported a long-term limiting illness or disability in the 2001 Census. 10.9 million people in the UK reported LTID, with significant regional variations (e.g. London and South East England: 15%; North East England: 23%).
[2] Figures for Wales not available for 2000/1 and 2003.
Source: Riddell et al., 2005

From marketisation to personalisation? New Labour and direct payments

Many of the key themes which linked direct payments to the broader agenda of marketisation under the Major Government have been developed through a more recent focus on the 'personalisation' of social care services from New Labour. This revisits familiar themes around the enhanced involvement of users in service delivery, upholding choice and control and increasing accountability (Leadbeater, 2004) and develops these by integrating a role for self-organisation and independent living within services. As chapter 6

Figure 1.1 Number of people receiving direct payments 2001–2005 by user group

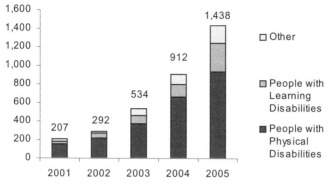

Source: Direct Payments Scotland 2005: Statistics Release (Scottish Executive, 2005a)

Figure 1.2 Number of people receiving direct payments in 2005 by user group and age

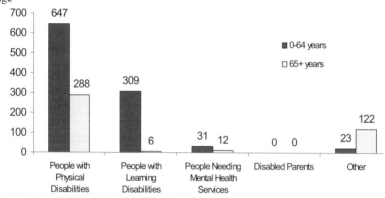

Source: Direct Payments Scotland 2005: Statistics Release (Scottish Executive, 2005a)

Figure 1.3 Value of direct payments by user group, 2001–2005

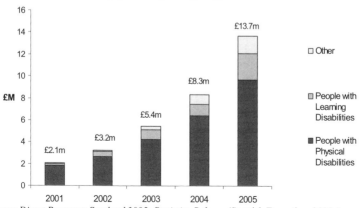

Source: Direct Payments Scotland 2005: Statistics Release (Scottish Executive, 2005a)

Figure 1.4 Number of people receiving direct payments in 2005 by local authority and user group

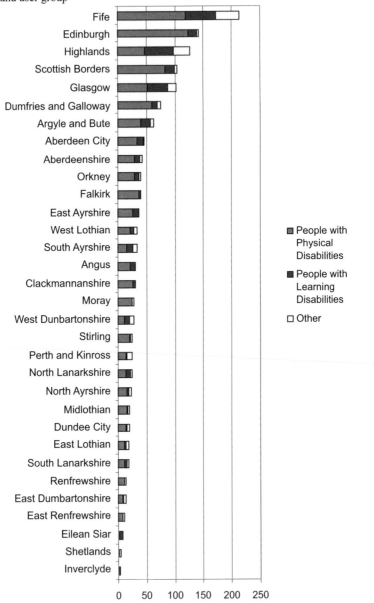

Source: *Direct Payments Scotland 2005: Statistics Release* (Scottish Executive, 2005a)

Figure 1.5 Rate of direct payment users per 10,000 population in 2005 by local authority

Source: Direct Payments Scotland 2005: Statistics Release (Scottish Executive, 2005a)

and discussion in the forthcoming chapters outlines, these themes have been organised into an agenda for service change in the publication *Improving the Life Chances of Disabled People* (Prime Minister's Strategy Unit et al., 2005). This strategy document clearly presents a significant future for the direct payments model and related support structures. However, there remain a number of challenges to address if this is to become manifest in practice. It is therefore hoped that this book will begin to set out some of these issues.

Conclusions

This chapter has introduced the background to the development of direct payments in Scotland. It is clear from the discussion that a number of factors have been highly significant in securing policy development. This has included challenges to existing service structures led by disabled people in Lothian, alongside a broader restructuring of support by central government through the ILT and ILF. The success of these early indirect payments, facilitated either through local authorities or through the ILF, clearly took many people by surprise and initiated a longer-term shift towards formal recognition of direct payments. Even from these early stages, negotiations for policy development remained ad hoc and were reliant on the perseverance of small groups of disabled people and their allies at central and local government levels. Since then, policy has sought to diversify user access, although the increase in take-up has been gradual. In chapter 2, we explore the way in which direct payments are understood within the micro-cultures of two Scottish local authorities.

Note
1. Award reference number: RES-000-23-0263.

Changing Cultures of Care in Scotland?
The Experience of Two Local Authorities

Charlotte Pearson

Introduction

Chapter 1 introduced the key themes to be addressed throughout this book and, more specifically, those emerging through the implementation of direct payments over the last decade in Scotland. This began by outlining the broad pattern of policy development and how this has reflected competing demands from the disability movement for the flexibility, control and empowerment enabled through direct payments, alongside their eventual promotion from successive Conservative and New Labour Governments within a broader agenda of marketised and personalised care. Discussion therefore highlighted both how direct payments have been promoted through activism in local areas as well as broader national trends, where earlier policies such as the ILF and ILT also allowed the advantages of personal assistance schemes to be seen.

However, since their implementation in 1997, it is clear that direct payments have only met with marginal success in Scotland. Whilst users have largely welcomed policy, many local authorities have been reluctant to promote them as a mainstream option. Using these themes, this chapter begins to explore the impact of these issues at the local level by comparing practice in two local authority case study examples. Discussion draws on data from a series of interviews and focus groups[1] conducted for the ESRC study with practitioners, users and related personnel (see appendices 2 and 3 for more details) and highlights two main themes. This begins by looking at the organisation of direct payments within each area and then links onto a more in-depth appraisal of changing cultures of social work. These themes and the experiences of these authorities are then revisited in the broader context of discussion on support organisations, marketisation and user experiences in chapters 3, 4 and 5.

The local authorities chosen for discussion highlight the diversity in approaches taken in adopting direct payments, as well as their impact in different geographical, and socio-economic locations. As shown in Table 2.1, local authority 1 was based in a rural area of Scotland. This included some of the richest neighbourhoods in Scotland, as well as some very deprived areas

Table 2.1 Summary of local authority characteristics

	Characteristics of authority	Overview of direct payments	Financial management	Views of social workers	Views of direct payments users	Support organisation perspective
Local authority 1	Rural area, some pockets of deprivation. Below UK median use of direct payments. No overall political control.	Positive synergy between LA and support organisation. Broad support from senior management – direct payments helpful for meeting needs in dispersed rural area. Desire for expansion in the future.	Devolved care management – widespread use of spot contacting.	Heavy reliance on support organisation for training, information and help with financial monitoring.	Increase in management of direct payments on behalf of severely disabled family member. Family members felt direct payments gave them greater control over quality of care. Needed extensive support from support organisation.	User-led management committee. Major support for direct payment users and social workers. Undertakes financial monitoring functions on behalf of LA.
Local authority 2	Urban area. Significant deprivation. Below UK median use of direct payments. Old Labour authority.	Lack of synergy between LA and support organisation. Official support from management, but many problems recognised. Managers believed more funds would be released for direct payments once demand demonstrated. Historical resistance from UNISON: direct payments seen as 'creeping privatisation'.	Resources tied up in home care and day services. Separate budget for direct payments which was overspent.	Generally resistant. Complaints about lack of training – denied by management. Many concerns: accountability for public money; risk of abuse of vulnerable children and adults; substandard care; practitioners' loss of control; LA liability; users' ability to manage funds; unfair treatment of personal assistants.	Direct payments seen as potentially transformative, but believed that LA wanted policy to fail. Support from CIL restricted because of waiting list.	Centre for Independent Living. Difficulty negotiating contract with LA. Believed LA lacked resources for and commitment to direct payments.

which have experienced long-term decline as a result of the collapse of the fishing industry. At the time of interviewing, the council was under no overall control. Interviews across the interest groups indicated that elected members were unlikely to know much about direct payments but would probably be broadly supportive of the underlying modernisation of welfare principles, as long as the financial stability of the local authority was not threatened. The authority had a below median number of direct payments users per 10,000 population. However, there had been a four-fold increase in the number of users since 2001 and in the overall value of payments allocated. Around two-thirds of users were recorded as having physical disabilities. The remaining group consisted mainly of people with learning difficulties and a smaller cohort of 'other' users (this included people with mental health problems, older people and parents of disabled children).

In contrast, local authority 2 was an urban area with some affluent pockets but also some of the most socially disadvantaged neighbourhoods in Europe. As a result of the long-term decline of traditional industries, a very high proportion of the population was economically inactive. The council was Labour-led and, like local authority 1, was recorded as having below median use of direct payments, and a similar increase in direct payments use and value since 2001. Around half of the total number of users were recorded as having physical disabilities.

The following section begins by exploring how local authorities have organised direct payments within their existing community care frameworks. Discussion highlights some of the tensions emerging from different forms of contracting and attempts by management teams to implement direct payments alongside existing service arrangements. This then moves on to discuss the impact of these changes on the culture of social work in each area.

Introducing direct payments: reorganising local cultures of care

As suggested so far, direct payments met with a slow start in their implementation. Whilst the 1996 Act enabled local authorities to progress with the development of schemes, it is clear that the shift to mandatory implementation from 2003 has been the main impetus to policy development in Scotland (this is explored in more detail in chapter 4).

Indeed, this pattern of availability was reflected in both case study areas and, although some practitioners had heard about policy since the outset, 2003 was generally the most common time for more general awareness among staff.

Overall, senior managers in both areas were broadly supportive of the policy ethos and suggested that the shift towards user empowerment enabled through direct payments was to be welcomed. As stated in chapter 1, implementation of direct payments by the Conservative Government, as part of the broader reorganisation of community care from the mid-1990s, envisaged that direct payments would be offered as an alternative to other service options. In turn it was stipulated that this should not be a preferential or more expensive option than directly provided services (Scottish Executive, 1997). However, both of these issues were raised as concerns by different levels of staff. In local authority 2, there were broader reservations from some frontline staff over the role of direct payments as an alternative to more traditional services. As one respondent commented:

> I feel a lot of people go for a direct payment because it is more flexible and it is the only option to inflexible traditional services. (social worker, local authority 2)

Moreover, senior managers in local authority 1 suggested that direct payments could be a more expensive option over the longer term as there were a number of hidden costs, such as funding a support organisation and monitoring payments, to take into account. Furthermore, accountability of public money was inevitably a key challenge for the local authority, but one that may be problematic within the existing social service structures:

> it's a new way of doing things, and doesn't fit into ... the bureaucratic side of the local authority terribly well. (senior manager, local authority 1)

Indeed, contrasts in the broader financial organisation of direct payments in each area underpinned some of the wider issues of local policy implementation. In local authority 1, direct payments had been integrated as part of the wider community care system. This centred around a system of devolved care management, whereby social workers were able to spot purchase services on behalf of users. As one of the senior managers commented, the development of direct payments could be linked in and complement this system of contracting:

> We've always had care managers who are ... financially literate, or we hope they are anyway. We have a fairly high degree of delegation to the front line in terms of money, so the care managers are actually able to make decisions themselves on the use of money and are expected to maintain and monitor their own budgets. (senior manager, local authority 1)

However, in authority 2 a designated cash-limited budget had been set aside for direct payments, so they did not impact on the financing of other services. This meant that direct payments were not set up as a mainstream service option and instead were restricted by a waiting list. The lack of available funds was acknowledged by managers to have been a major factor in the limited uptake of direct payments. As a result, the budgetary constraints and the perceived extra work associated with the policy led one respondent to comment:

Because of budget pressures and the amount of work that you have to do to process the direct payment, I wonder if some people are avoiding fully promoting it. (team leader, local authority 2)

It was, however, hoped that this was not the case, and senior management had advised all care managers that they should continue putting in applications and that money would be made available as payments were approved.

Social workers, on the other hand, were very clear that lack of money and the resulting waiting lists were the biggest restriction on the development of policy. As one practitioner told of her experiences:

I've been trying personally to support a couple of my workers to get a direct payment since April. One of the ladies was terminally ill. She's not going to make it before she gets the payment. And that doesn't feel good. (social worker, local authority 2)

In this context, it appeared unlikely that the authority's directly provided services would be significantly reorganised over the longer term, as they were tied into block contracts (this issue is revisited in more detail in chapter 4). It was therefore anticipated that new users would move from an existing service to direct payments, thus freeing up funds rather than implementing a broader structural reorganisation of services. However, as noted earlier, it was thought that the implementation of direct payments had in fact caused more people to enter the community care system, thus creating even greater demand. As one team leader explained:

We have had lots of people who've stayed away from our door because they didn't want our services, but with the option of having a direct payment, want to [deal] with us, so it has generated demand for a direct payment service, but it hasn't freed up people moving across. (team leader, local authority 2)

It was suggested by the Finance Officer in local authority 2 that direct payments would come to be accepted as another way of receiving a service, particularly in teams such as learning difficulties that already had a good commissioning system. But she was concerned that in other areas, any reorganisation of services in favour of direct payments would result in funds being taken away from services that benefited larger numbers of people. This would occur because the unit cost of providing a direct payment was higher than the unit cost associated with providing a direct service such as a day centre or home care.

Renegotiating roles: challenges to social work cultures

As will be noted in chapter 4, the role of social work staff as gatekeepers to direct payments has been well documented (Stainton, 2002). Indeed, research to date has presented something of a mixed picture when looking at these roles, highlighting not only examples of good practice (Clark et al., 2004), but also a substantive critique on what many have seen as a conflict of values between social work culture and the principles of independent living promoted by the disability movement throughout their campaign for direct payments (Pearson, 2006). This section of the chapter explores some of these issues by looking specifically at the impact of direct payments on the changing roles and responsibilities of frontline practitioners.

In local authority 1, practitioners also raised concerns relating to the potential impact of direct payments on existing services. However, more specific issues were voiced around the increased financial monitoring required with direct payments and the additional roles associated with these tasks. As a result, these were seen to challenge the more traditional responsibilities of social workers.

Indeed, many of the practitioners interviewed were wary about the loss of control over services through the availability of direct payments and voiced concerns over their increased financial management responsibilities:

> I personally resented the notion that I would be checking invoices for services that I had not commissioned. (care manager, local authority 1)

> I'm a social worker, I'm not a finance person and we already have quite a heavy responsibility in our work. I thought that part of the process wasn't appropriate to me. (social worker, local authority 1)

This linked into wider issues over the accountability of direct payments – in terms both of assessing a person's ability to manage the payments and of the practitioner's responsibility for monitoring them. As one care manager asked:

> How do you determine if somebody's capable of managing [the direct payment]? I mean we've had people that have been made bankrupt in the past and are now receiving direct payments and if they were bankrupt in the past, they obviously couldn't manage . . . are we trained to determine whether or not they are now capable? (care manager, local authority 1)

In contrast, other social workers in the authority saw the assessment of individual capability as an integral part of their job. Therefore assessing a person's ability to manage a direct payment was not viewed as a major difficulty.

However, senior managers in local authority 1 were clearly concerned that the monitoring role was not as strict as it could be, reflecting the view from practitioners that it was an excessive burden for them to undertake. As a result, the authority was looking to remove this area of responsibility from social workers and make it an extended remit for the support organisation. Again this is an area that will be revisited in chapters 3 and 4 by looking specifically at the role of the local support organisation.

In local authority 2, social worker views of direct payments were perhaps more mixed. As suggested, their role as a means of enabling more person-centred services was largely welcomed. Yet senior managers conceded that the reactions of some practitioners in training sessions had not been quite so positive, with one respondent commenting:

> the whole idea of service users having control I think brought people out in a rash. (team leader, local authority 2)

But as in local authority 1, accountability of direct payments had also emerged as a key concern. Indeed, the finance officer emphasised the need to establish a balance between monitoring public money and enabling optimum flexibility to allow the user to make the most of the payment. Implementation of direct payments to date has highlighted confusion from both users and practitioners over what payments can be used for (see Pearson, 2000), and in this authority examples of misuse included the purchase of theatre tickets and lunches out. However, it was stated that even in these cases the boundaries were unclear and the authority would investigate the individual circumstances rather than immediately suspending the direct payment.

Practitioners in authority 2 also expressed concerns about the accountability and monitoring of the use of direct payments. This raised broader questions about control and who the direct payment was intended for (this will be returned to later in this chapter). As one care manager explained:

> I think one of the biggest difficulties occurs when carers really are quite desperate for the direct payment. Your assessment may be that there's an ulterior motive for it. I work in an area – a very poor area, poverty is rife. And there's quite a few cases where it's an income to the family and in those cases we'll say no. (care manager, local authority 2)

Whilst senior managers in local authority 1 were examining alternative ways of managing the financial monitoring of direct payments by using the support organisation to take on this role, in local authority 2 the public sector union, UNISON, had become involved to challenge what was perceived as increased responsibilities. Indeed, at one point the union had advised its members not to process direct payments. Whilst the action was quickly resolved, broader questions over the role of direct payments have remained.

These concerns were picked up in an interview with the local UNISON representative. As he explained, direct payments were viewed by the union as a move towards privatisation which would inevitably lead to job losses for existing council workers. Although at the time of interviewing he was not aware of any specific complaints about direct payments, the idea of giving cash to service users to buy in services raised concerns over the pay and conditions of personal assistants and a downgrading of these roles. A comparison was made with another form of direct payment – Attendance Allowance[2] – where it was suggested that problems had previously arisen with recipients paying for cash-in-hand support, rather than home helps. This had left the union feeling 'hostile' to any suggestion that service users might be given money to purchase their own services. These concerns have also been reiterated in policy briefings to members (see UNISON Scotland, 2004)

Conversely, in local authority 1 the UNISON representative for the area stated that issues regarding direct payments had not been raised locally, although she was aware that they were seen as being more controversial in other areas.

However, some of the practitioners in local authority 2 had suggested that direct payments had in fact had a positive impact on their role, particularly in cases where users had had negative experiences with more traditional services. One practitioner spoke about two of her clients who had regularly taken out on her their frustrations with the home care service, but had been much happier since receiving a direct payment. Whilst this example illustrates one of the more successful transitions to direct payments in the local authority, it underlines a problem with using policy for 'difficult cases' rather than a mainstream option for all those in receipt of a community care assessment.

Indeed, significant reservations were expressed about the broader implementation strategy and what was felt to be a lack of commitment to policy in the local authority and the financial restrictions associated with a separate cash-limited budget. As one practitioner commented:

> We're not naïve, we realised that it would be based on budgets and stuff as well. And that's where the frustration is coming in. Because in some respects we feel that perhaps there just isn't the money in the system for it. And I would rather they just said that. (social worker, local authority 2)

Discussion in chapter 4 will also highlight some of the broader problems with access to social work training and information around direct payments across local authorities in Scotland. This was a key concern impacting on practice in local authority 2. From a senior management perspective, the importance of training and information was underlined, and it was emphasised that this had been available to all staff. However, several practitioners contradicted this view and a perceived lack of training emerged as a key source of frustration for them. It was suggested that initial training was offered to senior social workers, with more junior staff given a 'briefing' rather than a full training course. Indeed, one practitioner said that she had received an application for direct payments before she had received any training. Another asked if she could attend a training course but was told that this was only available to practice team leaders.

Indeed, the lack of training emerged as a source of frustration for several of the social work staff and, when combined with the extra paperwork involved, meant that processing a direct payment had had a significant impact on their workload. Furthermore, there was doubt about the accuracy of some of the information given to social workers, which had also led to a lack of confidence in the service. As one social worker commented:

> It's been patchy, it's been inconsistent, we've actually been given wrong advice and it's really contributing to muddying the waters for us ... we're finding it really frustrating right now. (social worker, local authority 2)

There were clearly differences among social workers in the authority with regard to the level of interest in direct payments. For example, a senior social worker thought that this was one of the main reasons why there had not been a significant demand to move away from traditional services. However, other practitioners thought that interest among their clients was high, although there were some groups such as older people who were thought to be less keen. This view was also reflected in local authority 1, where one care manager explained a possible reason for low uptake by older people:

> For our clients generally the carers are providing an awful lot of hands-on, everyday care ... the families of our clients are working very hard already, possibly that contributes to the fact that they don't want the extra responsibility. (care manager, local authority 1)

Overall, the profile of the users who practitioners considered to be the main beneficiaries of direct payments revealed significant differences between the local authorities. Whilst staff in both areas identified younger adults as the most likely potential users, many of the new users in local authority 1 were parents of a disabled child. On the one hand, it was expected that the direct payment would be maintained with the child as they moved into adult services. However, at this stage there appeared to be a more general view among practitioners that direct payments were most likely to work if their management was shared with another person. As discussion in chapter 5 highlights, this raises broader questions about the 'ownership' of the direct payment and its position as a means to facilitate independent living.

These issues return to broader concerns relating to the culture of social work. Indeed, this was identified by managers in local authority 2 as one of the main challenges of practice. It was hoped that, as existing staff were trained and new social workers came into the system, attitudes would change. It was also recognised that the expectations of some service users would need to change if policy was to be successful. As one team leader commented:

> I think it's a culture of dependence that we have created, we as a society, you know, that people are dependent on services. They've been made dependent on services, and so they become less able to problem solve for themselves. (team leader, local authority 2)

Staff therefore anticipated that this would change over time, particularly as young disabled people moved through the system. The team leader explained:

> I think as young people with a disability have better education and better life options, you know, horizons, who have a voice, then they're more ready to be independent and take the responsibilities along with it.

However, staff in both local authorities questioned the appropriateness of older people taking full responsibility for a direct payment as they were accustomed to receiving services.

Conclusion

This chapter has introduced some of the key themes and debates which arose in the case study local authorities examined. At this stage, discussion focused on the organisation of direct payments within each area and some of the challenges to social work roles.

When looking at the positioning of direct payments within existing community care systems, two contrasting responses from the case studies were highlighted. In local authority 1, the use of spot contracting through devolved care management was felt to be helpful in allowing the local authority more flexibility in decision-making over care packages and assessments for direct payments. Conversely, in local authority 2 senior staff ensured that other services were not affected by direct payments, by setting aside a separate budget. However, the cash limits placed on this resulted in the introduction of a waiting list for potential users. This has clearly limited the scope for mainstream access to direct payments in the local authority. However, in both areas the limited use of policy has meant that a major restructuring of services has not yet been required. This theme is revisited in chapter 4 by looking at the broader pattern of service reorganisation in Scotland as a whole.

Implementation of direct payments clearly raises a number of challenges for social workers as they accommodate new roles and responsibilities. In this chapter, these have been explored in the context of increased financial monitoring, accountability and the ways in which the two case study authorities have addressed these changes. Likewise, issues relating to training frontline staff in taking on these roles have also highlighted gaps in practice. As noted, these will be explored in further detail in the forthcoming chapters, in the context both of the case studies and of other examples from across local authorities in Scotland.

Notes

1. In order to protect the anonymity of local authority staff, specialist job titles have been replaced with more generic terms such as 'senior manager' or 'team leader'.
2. Attendance Allowance is a social security benefit paid from central government to people over the age of 65 who are assessed as requiring additional support with personal care.

CHAPTER 3

Supporting Roles

Charlotte Pearson

Introduction

The role of support organisations has been highlighted as a critical factor in the successful implementation of direct payments by government (see, for example, Scottish Executive, 2003a) and users alike (Evans and Hasler, 1996; Hasler et al., 1999). Indeed, from the outset of campaigning, centres for independent/integrated living (CILs) have been instrumental in developing community-based support controlled by disabled people. However, as a wider network of support has developed, there remain tensions as to the type of organisation local authorities have chosen to take on to deliver these roles and expectations about service delivery. This chapter will explore these key debates by looking at the issues around support that have developed in Scotland. Discussion will draw on the existing literature in this area and will be supplemented by findings from the telephone interviews and case study data of two Scottish local authorities from the ESRC study.

Models of support: developing a user-led approach in Scotland

As direct payments have developed over the past decade, support organisations have become increasingly important as integral parts of these schemes. Their roles in raising awareness and providing assistance to those using or considering a direct payment have clearly enabled wider policy use. Indeed, analysis for the ESRC study showed that support schemes undoubtedly have a positive impact on direct payments use, encouraging take-up by up to 80% when tested at UK level (Riddell et al., 2005). Furthermore, there appears to be a direct correlation between high take-up and the presence of support schemes run by user-led organisations. Whilst practical issues such as payroll and administration of direct payments are potentially transferable, support organisations run by disabled people are credited with a better understanding of key issues and have increasingly developed peer support networks (see Barnes and Mercer, 2006). However, as findings from this chapter indicate, this relationship may also be mediated by issues of funding, competition in a developing 'support market' and relationships with the purchasing authority.

In Scotland, support roles for direct payments have been led by the two CILs. These organisations opened in the 1990s, beginning with the Lothian Centre for Integrated Living in 1991 and followed by the Centre for Independent Living in Glasgow (now renamed Glasgow Centre for Inclusive Living, or GCIL) in 1995. Both the Edinburgh and Glasgow centres offer a range of peer-led services focused around the independent living needs of disabled people and, together with the Scottish Personal Assistants Employers Network (SPAEN), they form the major centres of user-led expertise for direct payments north of the border (Pearson, 2004b).

Recognition of the poor uptake of direct payments in Scotland from 1997 (see Witcher et al., 2000) led to a more concerted push from the Executive to encourage local authorities to develop policy and seek out accompanying support organisations. Hence, as well as expanding user groups and setting out the shift to mandatory implementation through the Community Care and Health (Scotland) Act 2002, earlier provisions were made to set up the Direct Payments Scotland (DPS) project in 2001. An initial allocation of £530,000 was made, with renewed funding until its closure in December 2005. The remit of the project covered three main areas. Two of these were increasing awareness of direct payments among users, local authority staff and service providers and the identification of training needs. The third area focused more specifically on developing support organisations – with the adoption of a user-led approach as the recommended format.

When DPS was first set up in October 2001, only five support organisations were in place, covering seven local authorities (DPS, 2005). Since then, this number has increased significantly and by 2005 it had increased to 14, covering 22 areas. Throughout this time, DPS worked closely with the two CILs and promoted their approaches to user-led support as a model for service development throughout their practice guidance (see DPS, 2002). Whilst findings from the ESRC study confirmed that most local authorities found DPS largely helpful in their role, this approach to encouraging local support structures differed considerably from government-led initiatives elsewhere in the UK. Support in Northern Ireland has been centred around the work of the Centre for Independent Living in Belfast, with funds made available from HSS in the Province. In Wales, limited funds for support have been targeted at local authorities rather than organisations themselves (Pearson, 2006). Notably, as discussion in the next section outlines, in England a concerted effort was made to channel a designated stream of funding into new support groups. This was organised through a development fund which was led by the Department of Health.

The experiences of the Direct Payments Development Fund in England

By looking at the process of developing support structures in England, a broader focus on the type of options available for these roles can be explored. From 2003, a funding pool of £9 million was made available over three years to encourage investment in direct payments support services. As Hasler (2006) points out, it was decided that monies should be allocated through grant aid to voluntary organisations, rather than allocating it directly to local authorities. This therefore established a separation of these roles and secured their independence from the local authorities. In order to qualify, organisations had to show that they were working in partnership with their local authority and that there was an implementation plan to increase take-up of direct payments. Funding was made through two rounds which gave each project an 18-month budget.

Clearly, the development fund model differs from the DPS strategy employed by the Scottish Executive in that additional monies were made available in local areas to actually develop support structures. Although this was organised through a bidding process and therefore meant that not all areas received funds for development, it remained the only example in the UK of targeted funding for support through the availability of additional funds. Indeed, the absence of earmarked funds for support organisations was cited as a common complaint by both Scottish and Welsh authorities and health and social service trusts in Northern Ireland throughout the telephone interviews. Given this concern, the Scottish Executive have since announced additional finance of £1.8 million for direct payments in 2006-07 and £2 million during the following year, and the development of support organisations has been stipulated as one of the priorities for this funding (DP News, 2005). In addition, as detailed in chapter 6, new grants have been made available to different interest groups to enable specialised support to develop across new user groups over the next few years.

As Hasler (2006) explains, the type of organisations awarded monies through the Development Fund varied considerably in their size, ethos and focus. In the first round of grants, more than a third of funds were made to general projects, rather than those targeting a specific group. Only three targeted black and ethnic minority users, two focused on children and young people and one on blind people. In round two, the focus was more varied, with six targeting older people and 13 targeting a range of 'under-represented' groups such as people with learning difficulties, disabled parents and deaf-blind people. Furthermore the methods used also varied considerably. Whilst all projects included some information plans, other roles incorporated areas such as training, peer support, or some form of personal assistant recruitment.

This varied focus on general as well as specific user groups within support organisations in England has again differed from approaches north of the border. Whilst the ethos of organisational control may vary, support modes in Scotland have been led either by the expertise from the two main CILs – in the case of developing user-led approaches – or by more generic frameworks led by local authorities or other new non-user-led groups. In either case, support provision in local areas has tended to be framed around generic needs of all impairment groups or by specialised support within organisations. However, as earlier research has shown (see Pearson, 2004b), there remains a significant gap in the provision of culturally specific support for users in black and minority ethnic communities in Scotland, and even the CILs remain uneasy about their ability to provide specialised support across all user groups.

In line with the ESRC findings, research on the Development Fund initiatives also showed that projects reporting the biggest success in increasing take-up of direct payments were those which identified themselves as being 'user-led' and with a long-term commitment to independent living (Hasler, 2006). In contrast, Hasler highlights some of the problems with using more traditional voluntary sector organisations, where in one case, only one new user had entered the scheme after 12 months of work.

Whilst CILs have traditionally been seen as the main providers of independent living support and expertise around direct payments, the experience of the Development Fund demonstrates that a number of alternative support organisations have developed throughout the UK over the past few years. In these cases, groups are not led by users and the overall direction of services tends to be outwith broader principles of independent living. Indeed, looking at the wider UK picture, interview data from the ESRC study highlighted that in 2005 only one quarter of English authorities were contracting with a user-led organisation (see Priestley et al., 2006). Six (14%) were local authority-led and the remaining 26 (61%) contracted with voluntary sector organisations that were not user-led (although they sometimes employed disabled staff or had an advisory board of disabled people). The picture in Wales also showed a degree of resistance to the user-led model, with only two authorities contracting with user-led support groups (one of which at the time of interviewing was suspended pending a re-tendering process). In contrast, all the support offered to direct payments users by HSS in Northern Ireland had been arranged through the CIL in Belfast, with key workers covering support in six of the eight trusts interviewed (at the time of interviewing no formal support arrangements had been made by two trusts in the Northern Board area). Findings from Scotland also showed something of a mixed picture, with 13 out of 30 support services described as 'user-led'. In other areas, support was more generally run by voluntary organisations which were described as having 'user involvement' or had been developed 'in-house' through the local authority.

Developing a 'support market' in direct payments: issues for Scottish authorities

The increasing diversity in the structure and ethos of support organisations for direct payments therefore raises broader questions over the future development of these roles. On the one hand, the increase in the number of users facilitated through the shift to mandatory implementation should have provided a more secure long-term funding base for CILs and other user-led groups, as they have traditionally held the knowledge and expertise on direct payments. However, questions remain over both the funding base for these services and the commitment of local authorities to maintain support through this framework. Furthermore, as the earlier figures indicate, there has been an increasing challenge to their service provision in this area through the emergence of alternative non-user-led organisations, which in some areas have utilised opportunities to tender for baseline support from local authorities.

As already detailed, at the time of the telephone interviews 13 out of the 30 authorities in Scotland developed user-led support organisations in line with guidance set out by DPS and the Scottish Executive (DPS, 2002). In areas where the user-led model had not been used, a number of reasons were put forward by direct payment personnel to explain the alternative arrangements used. A third of authorities reported that they hoped a user-led ethos would eventually develop, with a view to full organisational control being secured as payments took hold. In these cases, lead direct payments practitioner personnel described in the telephone interviews how they sought to get local disabled people interested in developing a support organisation but without any success to date:

> It's just the reality of life in [the area] for disability work. For any group to form itself you've got to have a committed few to take it forward and I would say that despite what other people might say, I've seen no evidence of that. (lead direct payments practitioner, North Scotland)

In another case where the support tender had been taken on by a local carers centre, the respondent explained that the absence of overall user control was seen as unproblematic:

> It's not a concern for me because the carer centre [the support organisation] has demonstrated historically that they are user-focused. They are user-influenced and personally I see that as important as being user-led *per se*. We've locally had some debates with national people who argue a bit about 'Well where's your user-led organisation?' The fact is locally people aren't ready to take that on, but there are other ways of ensuring that appropriate support is there. (lead direct payments practitioner, East Scotland)

Two of the authorities where services had not been developed were in very rural localities. It was therefore suggested that the geographically dispersed populations made it difficult to get an organisation established or secure a tender from a group willing to take on the role. Similarly, in some of the island communities the notion of developing collective support by disabled people was questioned. As a lead direct payments practitioner in North Scotland commented, 'there's nothing like that up here'.

In several areas, this raised broader questions about the 'ownership' of direct payments by, and their historical importance to, disabled people. As discussed, although the role of disability activism has clearly been important in the development of direct payments and campaigning alliances between policy planners and disabled people have been critical in securing change, these relationships have only emerged in certain parts of the UK. This, in turn, appeared to have impacted on some local authorities' commitment to developing user-led support organisations and had encouraged alternative models of support to be pursued. Notably, in one area the significance of disabled people in securing change was acknowledged, but amid broader criticism of this role in service development. It was therefore suggested that:

> the continual will to promote their agenda is in conflict with developments across all care sectors. (lead direct payments practitioner, West Scotland)

Despite the commitment from the Scottish Executive to achieving user-led support organisations across Scotland, the absence of earmarked additional funding for these roles has clearly had a knock-on effect on the level of service offered. As reported elsewhere (Pearson, 2004b), the two main CILs and SPAEN have experienced considerable variation in local authority willingness to cover support for payments. This has ranged from councils who have made core funding through block contracts, to those who have made no or limited contributions. As d'Aboville (2006) describes, negotiations to secure contracts between local authorities and support organisations can be drawn out, with conflicting expectations between the two parties. For CILs in particular, negotiations for direct payments support funding can impact on broader campaigning and service provision roles. Writing as the Director of GCIL, d'Aboville explains that after several years of erratic funding, his main concern has been to secure a stable funding base for the organisation. This required the local authority to recognise the broader role of the organisation in developing independent living services for disabled people across housing, employment and transport, rather than simply providing a support service for direct payments users. For him, this tension between roles exemplified a wider problem in the implementation of direct payments, where he argues that:

> The focus of many initiatives seems to be on implementing direct payments almost for their own sake rather than on exploring the

many ways disabled people can be empowered to develop flexible forms of support and take control of their lives. (d'Aboville, 2006: 147)

It is therefore clear that local authorities have been reluctant to fund support for organisations like the CILs beyond a remit of direct payments. Wider campaigning roles and independent living service support have been received far less favourably. Indeed, at the time of writing, despite providing direct payments support across a number of nearby local authorities, LCIL, based in Edinburgh, had been forced to end one of its key areas of service provision – the Peer Counselling Service. Likewise, the National Centre for Independent Living (NCIL) in London was awaiting news on further funding as it neared the end of its grant from the Development Fund. As no additional funds had been forthcoming, redundancy notices had been issued to all staff and it remains unclear how independent living support and services will continue over the longer term.

The operation of support roles in the two case study authorities

In this section, discussion moves on to consider how supporting roles have been developed in the two case study authorities outlined in chapter 2.

Support for users in local authority 1 – a largely rural area but with some pockets of urban deprivation – was provided through a user-led organisation. Unlike the wider independent living remit of CILs, this group was set up solely to provide support for direct payments users in this and a neighbouring authority and had built up a body of employees able to visit direct payments users across the two areas. An initial contract had been awarded to the organisation for a three-year period and it was envisaged that this would be maintained on a rolling basis as user numbers increased. At the time of interviewing, the organisation supported approximately 40 users in the local authority area. The services offered were diverse in that they included payroll, assistance with recruitment and employment, advice on indemnity issues and pre-assessment support, alongside information support for local authority employees and accompanying social workers on visits to prospective users. This link between the local authority and the support organisation was clearly an important dimension of the group's remit and, as will be detailed below, presents a clear difference from local authority 2. Indeed, at the time of interviewing, the organisation was seeking to expand its role to include training for social workers and assistance with financial monitoring processes. This would be facilitated through a new part-time post created specifically to assist users with all monitoring issues. The aim of taking on the monitoring role was to reduce the workload of social work practitioners, who were generally unhappy at having to undertake this additional task on top of their existing responsibilities (see chapter 2).

Clearly this raises broader questions about the independence of the support organisation and the fragmentation of social work tasks, although some users had indicated that they had felt uncomfortable with practitioners conducting this role and felt that perhaps some 'distance' from the local authority would be preferable.

At the time of interviewing, competition for the support role had been limited to national bodies such as SPAEN and local groups keen to take on specific tasks such as payroll support. This was seen as largely unproblematic by the support organisation and not a major threat to service development.

In local authority 2 – an urban area – support was provided through the nearby CIL. In contrast with local authority 1, there had been a much longer period of involvement with direct payments, dating back to 1996 when support was provided for 100 indirect payments users. However, from 1996 to 2004, the development of this role had been limited, as the indirect scheme was frozen and no new direct payments (beyond a pilot scheme of 15 users) were made available. Again unlike local authority 1, the wider remit of the CIL has presented difficulties with the local authority in negotiating a contract. This has seen the CIL determined to maintain broader service development and campaigning roles for disabled people, whereas the local authority limited its commitment to financing a support service exclusively for direct payments users.

Therefore, despite the broader availability of expertise across a range of disability issues within the CIL, the support organisation in local authority 2 was contracted to undertake a more limited range of tasks. Notably, a system of support to social work staff had not been formally established, although advice would be given upon request and close links would be made with care managers as soon as the direct payment was in place. The CIL also provided some assistance with the monitoring of paperwork. However, the extent to which support staff should intervene in this role remained ambiguous, as some social work personnel were concerned that this level of intervention may simply indicate that a person was unable to manage the payment overall.

As in local authority 1, there was a gradual increase in alternative payroll services in the area and the CIL was aware that local businesses were increasingly seeking out the employment and management of personal assistants as a new opportunity. However, at the time of interviewing this had yet to become manifest as any direct threat to the CIL support role.

Conclusion: Direct payments, the 'support market' and the personalisation of care

As local authorities seek to develop their direct payments schemes, questions remain over the long-term direction and ethos of support roles. As the two examples from the case studies showed, even the user-led approach can differ within these frameworks of support, from newly established organisations set up with a specific remit to provide direct payments support to the CILs which have a long-term focus on campaigning and the provision of a wider network of independent living services. Evidence presented from the ESRC study may suggest that some local authorities are more comfortable in funding a designated service with a set number of roles (including those which have traditionally been covered by social work staff) rather than user-led organisations with a wider remit.

Other issues also look set to emerge. If the expansion of direct payments continues among 'new groups' such as older people and disabled children, these specialisations will also need to be developed by support organisations. Given that the model of support of CILs has been largely generated through the experiences of people with physical impairments, this is clearly an area where more diverse service development needs to be established. Over the next few years, there is some evidence to suggest that this will be an area where future work will occur. From 2007, support roles will be diversified through the allocation of Executive funds to develop specialist training for disabled children users, as well as a consortium of mental health organisations to deliver specialised support for mental health service users.

However, any shift towards a 'support market', where user-led roles are challenged by other organisations, may indeed conflict with broader policy goals from central government. January 2005 saw the publication of *Improving the Life Chances of Disabled People* (Prime Minister's Strategy Unit et al., 2005). Led by the Prime Minister's Strategy Unit with input from the Department for Education and Skills, the Department of Health, the Office of the Deputy Prime Minister and the Department for Work and Pensions, the document included a pledge to establish a user-led CIL in every local authority by 2010. In order to meet this commitment, it is clear that the current support models for direct payments will need to be maintained through user-led groups and, in line with the experiences of GCIL, the financial input from local authorities needs to integrate a wider range of independent living services. At the time of writing, it is unclear how this proposal will be developed in Scotland (this will be discussed further in chapter 6), but it does raise broader questions over the future of these roles.

CHAPTER 4

Direct Payments and the Marketisation of Care in Scotland

Sheila Riddell

Introduction

The restructuring of welfare, drawing on the principles of new public management, has been pursued by both Conservative and New Labour administrations. According to Clarke et al. (2000), a key feature of new public management is 'breaking down large scale organizations and using competition to enable "exit" or "choice" by service users'. The idea of users' rights to exercise choice in their use of public services has been promoted by individuals and groups at different positions on the political spectrum. Progressive self-help movements have argued for choice in order to achieve user empowerment, whilst neo-liberals have promoted choice as a means of promoting market-based solutions and curbing the powers of the state. This chapter explores a range of paradoxes arising in the development and use of direct payments for disabled people, and considers their implications for the development of social policy in Scotland post-devolution.

The involvement of the private and not-for-profit sectors in public service delivery is deeply contentious. For example, many commentators in the field of education see choice from a spectrum of service providers as a policy devised by the New Right to protect the interests of the middle class, even when the policy is disguised as offering new opportunities to disadvantaged groups. They suggest that new public management promotes a victim-blaming approach, so that poor educational and health outcomes may be blamed not on deficient services, but on the ill-advised choices of the poor. For example, much of the opposition to the Education Bill in England focused on measures to create independent trust schools funded by the local authority. The Scottish Executive has not, at the time of writing, signalled a major expansion in the role of the private or not-for profit sectors in the delivery of education north of the border. However, private sector involvement in state education in Scotland is evident in the financing of new school building through the Private Finance Initiative, the delivery of nursery education and the contracting out of services such as cleaning and school meals. In addition, schools involved in the Schools of Ambition programme have had to seek financial backing from the private sector, with organisations such as the Hunter Foundation making significant contributions. Notwithstanding these developments, the role of the private sector in the delivery of state education in Scotland has been relatively minor.

By way of contrast, within other social policy spheres, particularly community care, the 'mixed economy of welfare' has been promoted with considerable enthusiasm both north and south of the border. Community care policy was launched by the Conservative administration in the early 1990s with the stated objective of transforming public services, replacing outmoded institutions such as long-stay hospitals with community-based forms of provision and moving the prime focus from the interests of the service producer to those of the service user. Direct payments fitted relatively easily into the community care agenda, since the policy received the strong backing of the disability movement, because of its potential to promote independent living, and central government, wishing to modernise social care services. As discussed in this chapter, whilst some local authorities have embraced the modernisation agenda, this has been resisted equally strongly by others.

In order for direct payments to flourish within a mixed economy of care, a number of conditions have to be in place. On the demand side, there has to be a call for direct payments from people assessed as requiring community care services. On the supply side, there has to be sufficient scope within local authority budgets to make it possible to provide direct payments to those requesting them, as well as a sufficient supply of personal assistants to fill vacancies. In the following sections, we consider the factors which have contributed to the development of direct payments within the community care market, drawing on local authority respondent accounts and local authority case studies. This will include analysis from the telephone interviews conducted (see appendices for more details), alongside a focus on the operation of the market in each of the case studies outlined in chapter 2.

Existing services versus direct payments

One of the key barriers identified by local authority representatives concerns the impact of direct payments on existing service structures. As one planner commented:

> We aren't as financially well off as some local authorities and I know there were real financial concerns earlier this year. And that's about trying to provide the services that people still want traditionally and also providing direct payments too. (lead direct payments practitioner, East Scotland)

In another area it was suggested that even though there was a shift towards support for policy among more senior personnel and elected officials, there still remained significant areas of resistance within the department. As was explained, this centred on a rigid commitment to retain large block contracts within home care services:

> We have a big home care service within [the local authority] ... It's a council service and it's not been outsourced ... Whilst you've still got a huge amount of council service and workers employed there, it's a dilemma and certainly a tension. (lead direct payments practitioner, West Scotland)

Others conceded that although there was still some scepticism around direct payments, there were some changes:

> Things are slowly changing, an incremental thing, as people become more aware of ... as we become more involved with giving people direct payments you know the anxiety about them decreases to some extent. (lead direct payments practitioner, North-East Scotland)

The impact of local budgetary arrangements

It was evident that local contracting and budgetary arrangements had a major impact on the extent to which a market was able to develop. In general, local authorities with large block contracts tied up in existing services had far less freedom of movement, particularly when budgets were tightly stretched. Block contracts were often used to support services such as day centres for people with learning disabilities, which cost a certain amount of money irrespective of how many people were using them. Of course, there are pressures to review such services arising, for example, as a result of the review of services for people with learning disabilities *The Same as You?* (Scottish Executive, 1999), and this point is returned to in the conclusion of this chapter.

One respondent explained the salience of local budgetary arrangements thus:

> An awful lot of the applications we're seeing coming through are for people who are using existing service providers. They are not necessarily employing PAs. There's a reason for some of that. Again it comes back to the conflict we have and the tensions we have around other budget pressures, and certainly in relation to physical disabilities and learning disability you'll find that a good percentage of those clients are not receiving the council home care service, they're actually already receiving services from agencies and other service providers. And because of budget pressures on those particular packages, there has been a push towards moving

people out of those budgets and persuading them to maybe take a direct payment instead. (lead direct payments practitioner, West Scotland)

Consequently, this group of users often stayed with the same service provider or agency, with the implication that the experience of direct payments was different from that envisaged by the independent living movement:

> we have the bulk of the people in receipt of direct payments using agencies and not employing PAs. Now, you could argue that's not really what direct payments is about but equally, you could also argue direct payments is around choice and if people want to continue to use the agency that's fine. (lead direct payments practitioner, West Scotland

Reinventing direct payments? The impact of the 2003 changes

As described, the enabling framework for direct payments, which gave local authorities the option whether to develop schemes or not, clearly impacted on take-up in Scotland. Therefore the timing of the telephone interviews allowed us to explore whether the shift to mandatory implementation in 2003 had made significant changes to local policy development.

Perhaps unsurprisingly, 19 out of the 30 Scottish authorities interviewed (63%) reported that the 2003 changes had indeed acted as the main impetus to develop policy. As one respondent commented more generally, the impact had been vital to secure change:

> Without making it mandatory it would have been much slower ... I think all local authorities needed the coercion quite honestly. Left to their own devices, there'd still be far less direct payments throughout Scotland. (lead direct payments practitioner, East Scotland)

Even in other authorities where efforts had been made to implement policy from the 1996 Act, planners had found an overall lack of clarity on how to proceed with change, which in turn led many to give up:

> In '97 we rolled along with it ... there was so much initial confusion as to how you did it and the processes etc. and it never really took off. (lead direct payments practitioner, North-East Scotland)

Respondents in other areas stated that, although there may have been a few users with indirect payments, the absence of compulsion meant that no one was willing to take on the remit for direct payments and develop a local scheme.

Supply factors: the pool of personal assistants

The establishment of a successful market also depends on the existence of a sufficient body of workers willing to act as personal assistants, so the interviews with council representatives explored whether the local area had the capacity to supply the workers to meet these demands. Although many authorities reported an overall problem in terms of recruiting home care staff, over half indicated that this did not extend to direct payments. Whilst in some areas this was linked to the low number of users, other reasons for this pattern were seen as relating to the continuity of employment offered through direct payments, particularly when compared with home care. Furthermore, in several areas where difficulties had emerged, local authorities had raised their hourly rates to make personal assistance more attractive. As one respondent noted:

> Our experience has been that people have teething problems with personal assistants and then it settles down. Once they get the right person, they seem to manage to hold onto their staff ... Turnover for a lot of people is extremely low. (lead direct payments practitioner, North-East Scotland)

Knowledge and awareness of direct payments among social work staff

Clearly, social work staff are the 'street level bureaucrats' (Lipsky, 1980; Stainton, 2002) who have the power to encourage people to request direct payments or to deter them from this course of action. Their actions are likely to be guided by a number of factors, including knowledge and understanding of procedural matters, the extent to which they are convinced of the benefits of the policy to the individual and the system as a whole, and, perhaps most significantly, whether they believe it will have a negative impact on their personal workload. Support from the local authority through a range of means, including training, is essential in tipping the balance in favour of direct payments, so we asked council representatives about the information and training available to grass-roots staff.

In Scotland, although all areas had been involved in staff training, the approaches and intensity differed considerably. Notably, in authorities where designated direct payments posts had been developed, training strategies were far more ingrained in mainstream social work practice. For example, in one area the direct payments representative had spent time with all the care teams to inform them of changes. This was subsequently being developed as a rolling programme which involved all new staff. In another authority, a similar approach had been used and, as the respondent commented:

there's no excuse for anyone in the department not to know about direct payments. (lead direct payments practitioner, South-West Scotland)

In terms of targeting staff, despite attempts to integrate all care teams, community mental health practitioners and children's services were often cited as more difficult to involve.

In these areas, the impact of this training was clearly positive but as one respondent explained, there remained resistance from some staff over the broader principles of policy:

> I think the interesting thing is that once you get a worker involved in getting a direct payment up and running, they very quickly get two or three more. Whereas some people don't have anybody and you just know, even from the training, you know there are some people who just think it's all too risky and you can't let clients go down that road. (lead direct payments practitioner, North Scotland)

In other Scottish local authorities, training had been far less intense, with information conveyed through one-off events and ad hoc information sessions. Whilst these were generally organised from within the local authorities, there were examples where the support organisation and other key departments such as finance took a lead role. DPS also organised local events, particularly in some of the smaller northern and island authorities. Integrated approaches were also apparent, where direct payments training had been incorporated into wider training on single shared assessments and the Supporting People initiative.

In general, it was clear from the accounts of social workers in the case study local authorities that short, infrequent training sessions were often seen to be inadequate, and there was a perception, particularly in one authority, that initiating a direct payment was likely to result in a cumbersome bureaucratic process where the rules of engagement were unclear. Some local authority managers, on the other hand, felt that social workers overstated the lack of training, since the best way of increasing competence was not through training sessions, but by actually setting up direct payments packages in practice.

Regulating demand: publicising direct payments to potential users

Markets are clearly driven in large part by demand-side factors, and it was evident that, whilst expressing the view that there was only a limited client pool for direct payments, many local authorities were suppressing demand by withholding information or engaging in very limited publicity drives.

In the majority of Scottish local authorities, information leaflets and frontline staff were the most common publicity routes for potential users.

Voluntary sector organisations for and of disabled people were also used, as well as support organisations, as main points of contact. However, concerns were once again expressed about over-publicising the availability of direct payments because of the impact this might have on service budgets. As one lead practitioner commented:

> We did consider doing ... a media publicity on [direct payments]. We approached our media department on it but they felt at that stage that we really didn't have everything in place to be able to cope with the response ... and that we might be building up expectations of a service that we weren't quite ready to respond to. (lead direct payments practitioner, Central Scotland)

Examples of more innovative publicity drives emerged. For example, one local authority had produced a video specifically targeted at people with learning difficulties. It was felt that this had significantly increased the number of this group of users in the area.

Sometimes unexpected publicity for direct payments from an external agency had the effect of driving up demand, in a way which the local authority found difficult to control. For example, in one authority a small piece in a press release by DPS commented on low take-up in the area. The local media took up this story and it resulted in the Director of Community Care going on the radio to defend policy and budget overspend. As the interviewee stated:

> staff got the message that direct payments had been approved but there was no one to tell them to watch the cost. (lead direct payments practitioner, North Scotland)

This had caused considerable anxiety among service planners and concerns that direct payments had revealed 'hidden demand' for services which could not be met within existing budgets:

> Our services regulate themselves because some people won't want to come to a service where disabled people are. A lot of disabled people don't like disabled people, so they won't want to come. The same is true for people who are homeless or who are affected by domestic abuse. Being around other people in that area isn't what they choose so they opt not to have a service. So when you get cash instead it can release stigmas in people to say, 'I'll have some of that.' And that is the big problem for us to fund. (lead direct payments practitioner, North Scotland)

Despite some examples of local authorities making efforts to publicise the availability of direct payments in Scotland, a more common strategy was to keep the policy, at least to some extent, under wraps. Although the intention is for social workers to invite all those assessed as eligible for community care services to consider taking a direct payment instead of a council-run service, it was evident both from the interviews and from the local authority case studies that in practice this was not happening. Lack of a comprehensive campaign directed at potential users was one of the root causes of suppressed demand.

The impact of targets

A key assumption within new public management is that performance must be driven by the application of pre-specified targets, with less attention paid to micro-managing the process by which the outputs are achieved. We were therefore interested in the extent to which targets on uptake of direct payments were being used to drive the policy forward. The use of performance indicators and local targets for direct payments varies across the UK. In England, the Department of Health has used the proportion of direct payments users among community care users as a key indicator contributing to local authority star ratings, whilst less emphasis has been placed on targets in Scotland.

Indeed, only six of the Scottish local authorities had set some form of internal target for increased use of direct payments. In one area, this had only covered the first year of implementation. Four were more substantive, ranging from 100 users over three years through to aims for a 15% increase, and one was set specifically in relation to a Scottish Executive request to target older people as a key group. Almost all local authorities without targets set were resistant to them. Instead, they emphasised the need to shift the focus to ensuring users were fully informed about their service choices. One interviewee commented:

> our target is that everybody who gets a community care assessment is clear about what payments are and that we publicise it more and the support mechanisms are there for a wide range of people. (lead direct payments practitioner, West Scotland)

It was also felt that targets enforced more compulsion around direct payments, which would perhaps lead to users being forced to take on a direct payment when it was not the most appropriate service option.

However, in another area the absence of targets was seen negatively in terms of future policy development across different user groups:

> I would prefer to have clear targets. The targets would be for the area not for the client groups. We still have nine area teams, so typically I would be wanting to have been saying to the teams,

'Right, each of you need to be producing one direct payment per month' or similarly for every one hundred services established in any given period, 5% or so should be a direct payment. (lead direct payments practitioner, West Scotland)

Overall, it was evident that targets for increased use of direct payments were being used much less extensively in Scotland than in England, raising questions about whether this is one of the factors which has contributed to greater use of direct payments south of the border.

The place of direct payments within the constellation of services

Across Scotland, despite broader concerns over direct payments, the impact on existing services has, to date, been minimal. In most cases, authorities suggested that the number of users was not high enough to initiate a restructuring of services. As one respondent commented:

Direct payments are always going to be a minority service. (lead direct payments practitioner, North Scotland)

Another suggested that there had been anxieties around policy 'opening the floodgates' but conceded that this had not happened because:

people have to be fairly motivated to take up a direct payment. (lead direct payments practitioner, East Scotland)

However, there was a general level of concern over the long-term impact of policy. In one of the few areas where an impact on services was reported, the respondent stated that home care posts were already not being filled as a result of direct payments. As she commented:

more direct payments means less direct services. (lead direct payments practitioner, North-East Scotland)

This wider concern tended to emerge where service provision was organised through block contracts:

We are a big service provider, releasing resources takes time. We just don't have the money sitting in the bank in a sense to give people direct payments and it takes a while to create the sort of slippage. So [direct payments] coming without any [additional] money was a problem. (lead direct payments practitioner, North-East Scotland)

Therefore, rather than paying for direct payments from a unified service budget, local authorities were often having to find additional monies to support new users. This often reflected broader political resistance to direct payments in some authorities:

> People are just not able to get their heads around [direct payments]. Particularly in relation to making that final move on re-directing budgets and downsizing. I mean deliberate downsizing of existing services ... We seem reluctant to do that here ... We've made very small inroads into day care services, which is not what most direct payment users want. They want home care. (lead direct payments practitioner, West Scotland)

In this local authority, the presence of a large home care service meant that any direct payments where equivalent 'home care' needs were assessed could not be funded through the home care budget as this was tied up in a large block contract.

Conversely, two authorities used a system of spot contracting as part of their wider community care services. Consequently, this had allowed considerably more flexibility in accessing payments. Indeed, restructuring amid the community care reforms from April 1993 resulted in a system of spot contracting which was then used for direct payments. Therefore, despite still retaining a significant amount of home care provision within the local authority, the more flexible contracting systems meant that service commissioning for direct payments remained largely unaffected.

Increasing take-up: exploring the impact of directives from the centre

As suggested in chapter 1, the shift to mandatory implementation of direct payments in April 2003 has played a significant role in increasing policy take-up in Scotland. In England, its impact has been more varied, particularly in areas where authorities had been implementing direct payments for some time (Priestley et al., 2006). However, as in Scotland, the 2003 changes had proved pivotal in Northern Ireland, where the 1996 Act had been very poorly received, with only two out of the 12 trusts developing any local policy on direct payments. Likewise, implementation of the mandatory duty in Wales in 2004 has also been fundamental in challenging previously reluctant local authorities to adopt direct payments.

Other forms of encouraging take-up of direct payments have been used to different effect across the UK. As noted previously, in England since 2003 the Department of Health has included direct payments as a key performance indicator, which in turn affected local authorities overall 'star rating' (Priestley et al., 2006). Whilst this clearly impacted on take-up in England, elsewhere in the UK performance indicators have been largely resisted. In

Scotland, only six out of the 30 local authorities questioned (20%) used any form of local target and most areas were strongly resistant to any change. A similar level of scepticism was found in Wales, and in Northern Ireland no indicators had been established by the Department of Health, Social Services and Public Safety, although one trust had its own targets in place.

As discussion elsewhere suggests (Priestley et al., 2006), in tackling the problem of local resistance to direct payments it is clear that the introduction of mandatory duties and targets has made an impact. However, as Priestley et al. note, whilst a more centralist and managerialist approach to governance can impact positively on equity of access to direct payments for disabled people, questions may be raised as to the appropriateness of replicating other initiatives in each part of the UK. Although the shift to mandatory implementation enabled something of a policy re-launch for policy in areas outwith the traditional direct payments heartlands in the south of England, it is questionable whether what Priestley et al. calls characteristically 'English' solutions to policy implementation in local government through the use of performance indicators would meet with the same results elsewhere in the UK.

The operation of the market in two case study authorities

In this section, we consider the impact of the community care market on the development of direct payments in the two case study local authorities introduced in chapter 2.

Local authority 1 had begun to expand its use of direct payments significantly, particularly for older people and disabled children. The local authority had difficulty in delivering council care services in large parts of the authority, partly because of the large area and dispersed population. Agencies were also relatively thin on the ground. Direct payments were therefore congruent with the desire to expand services and draw in a wider range of care workers throughout the authority, not just in the urban centres. Care managers were not constrained by the authority's prior commitment to large block contracts, and generally expressed confidence in the assessment system which was used to decide whether a person was able to manage a direct payment. As described in chapter 3, the support organisation was led by disabled people, who made up the majority of the management board, but its focus remained exclusively on direct payments rather than a wider campaigning role. Services offered, including payroll and assistance with recruitment and employment, broadly matched the framework of support provided elsewhere but, as mentioned previously, the likely expansion of the organisation to include financial monitoring and social worker training looked set to establish alternative roles for the organisation. This reflected a wider confluence of interests between the local authority and the support organisation, with the community care market generally favouring the growth of direct payments.

In local authority 2, the picture was somewhat different. With a high proportion of extremely deprived people, there was a high demand for council services and budgets were tightly stretched. Significant funds were committed to block contracts with domiciliary care services, and there were also large commitments to traditional day centre provision for various groups. Council staff varied in their assessment of the extent to which direct payments were being promoted. According to senior managers and care commissioners, the level of funds available for direct payments would expand with increased demand from service users. However, grass-roots social work staff believed that the funds were not available and also complained about a very top-heavy signing-off system. This meant that requesting a direct payment was extremely labour intensive, and was likely to be met by a delay through admission to a waiting list. As a result, they felt it was better to dampen rather than raise expectations among potential users. In addition, they were concerned about potential users' ability to manage payments, the dangers of employing unsuitable personal assistants and loss of control over the quality of care delivered. A further limiting factor was the suspicion of direct payments evinced by UNISON, the principal public sector trade union. The union representative was anxious about social worker workload and also the terms and conditions of employment of personal assistants, which were worse from those enjoyed by directly employed council staff. Support was delivered in the main by a CIL, which also had a campaigning remit. Negotiating a working contract with the local authority had proved problematic, and as a result there had in the past been a waiting list of direct payments users requiring support. This again served to depress demand among potential users.

Comparing the cases of local authorities 1 and 2, it is evident that in the first local authority direct payments were able to grow, partly because they were not having to compete with firmly entrenched traditional services supported by block contracts. The activities of the support organisation and the local authority were generally well synchronised, with the support organisation taking over many of the roles which might elsewhere be undertaken by the local authority, such as training of social work staff, direct payments users and financial monitoring. By way of contrast, in local authority 2 a 'mixed economy of care' had failed to develop for a range of reasons including a protectionist approach to existing services, resistance by social work staff to an increased workload in launching the scheme, a fear that disabled people would be unable to manage funds effectively, lack of information at all levels and some degree of tension between the local authority and the support organisation.

Conclusion: direct payments, the welfare market and social justice

As we have seen, direct payments were achieved as a result of a struggle between the disability movement, local authorities and the state. At first resisting direct payments, the UK Government then came to realise that, aside from the independent living objectives, direct payments accorded well with its goals of modernising services and fostering a mixed economy of care. Local authorities have also adopted different positions, some resisting the policy and others pushing for even greater power to devolve funds to service users. So far, despite a rapid increase in use in Scotland from a very low base, the impact of direct payments has been limited, and there are large variations in the operation of the welfare market by local authority and user group. As the next chapter highlights, some users have found that direct payments have enabled them to realise some of the principles of independent living, whilst for others bureaucratic constraints, the power of gatekeepers and low levels of funding have made the experience of direct payments less than liberating. However, the future is unwritten, and direct payments may offer a new model of welfare delivery to be applied across the board.

With regard to the operation of the market within the delivery of public sector services, direct payments offer an interesting case of a policy which has been promoted by a minority group struggling for greater independence, who have come to see state services not as supportive but as oppressive. In areas such as education, enhancing individual choice has often been seen as regressive rather than progressive, whereas in the field of direct payments the exact opposite has been the case. This suggests that there is a need for some sections of the left to re-examine their blanket condemnation of the use of markets in the delivery of public services, since it would appear that under some circumstances the mixed economy of care may be able to deliver improved, if still imperfect services.

CHAPTER 5

The Views and Experiences of Direct Payments Users

Victoria Williams

Introduction

Discussion in chapter 1 set out both how the campaign for direct payments was driven by disabled people and how this impacted on activism and policy change in Scotland. Drawing on a number of these themes, this chapter moves on to explore the experiences and views of users of direct payments since initial implementation of the 1996 Act and more recent legislative change. The chapter begins by exploring how access to policy has been negotiated by different user groups and then is followed by a more in-depth appraisal of users' direct experiences, drawing on findings from the two case study authorities.

Negotiating user access to direct payments

As detailed in chapter 1, access to early indirect payments schemes was sporadic across the UK and was largely available only to people with physical impairments. This imbalance between user groups was reflected in a consultation paper from 1996, where a preference to provide direct payments to those with physical impairments under the age of 65 was indicated. However, after campaigning by People First and Values into Action, groups representing people with learning difficulties (Williams and Holman, 2006), the Act did include these potential users, but the age limit of 65 remained in place at this stage. Attempts were also made to exclude mental health service users from the policy, although these too were unsuccessful (Glasby and Littlechild, 2002). However, there was little in the guidance about implementing direct payments for this group or acknowledgment of additional barriers they might face accessing the policy, such as a lack of knowledge about the policy among service users or staff and a perception among potential users and staff that this group might be less able to manage money or staff, particularly when ill, resulting in increased support needs. (Glasby and Littlechild, 2002; Ridley, 2006)

There are few people with mental health problems using direct payments in the UK, which appears to confirm these assumptions, so the problem of low take-up has become self-perpetuating. However, accounts of direct payments users with mental health problems illustrate how successful the policy can be when it is implemented appropriately and imaginatively (Glasby and Littlechild, 2002; Ridley, 2006). Whilst the enabling feature of the 1996 Act made it easier for local authorities to restrict access to key groups, the numbers of users with learning difficulties and with mental health problems have remained low (see chapter 1 for more details).

The upper age limit for direct payments was removed in England, Wales and Scotland in 2000, making the policy available to older people. Later guidance from the Department of Health in 1999/2000 for England and Wales emphasised that the policy should be made equally available to all adult user groups, thereby reinforcing support for users with learning difficulties and mental health problems, the groups which had previously fared so poorly. Following this, direct payments were made available to the parents or guardians of disabled children in 2000 and to 16- and 17-year-olds in 2001. Legislation in 2001 made it mandatory to implement direct payments from April 2003. In Scotland, the Executive matched these changes in the Community Care and Health Act (Scotland) 2002, which required local authorities to implement the policy from June 2003. Thus all disabled people requiring a community care service have the option of receiving this service as a direct payment unless deemed ineligible.

The late inclusion of people with learning difficulties in the policy planning process after the earlier attempts to exclude them 'was one of the first stumbling blocks that contributed to the lack of suitable support schemes and structures for this group' (Williams and Holman, 2006: 67). The importance of ongoing support was highlighted in a report by Gramlich et al. (2002), which indicated that informal support from social networks and family could be as important as formal support, such as micro boards (small groups of people formally committed to providing support and planning for the disabled person) or that from support organisations. Findings such as these perhaps make it harder for practitioners to accept that direct payments can be a suitable method of service provision for people with learning disabilities, particularly if appropriate formal support is not clearly available, despite the allowance within the policy that the payment can be managed with as much support as necessary.

The stipulation that direct payments users should be 'willing and able' to manage the policy perhaps caused problems for practitioners who could not imagine how people with learning difficulties, or indeed mental health service users, could demonstrate that they were willing to take on the payment and were able to manage. Indeed the phrase is liable to an 'all or nothing' interpretation and, in the case of mental health service users, it is assumed that the user must both employ personal assistants and take full financial responsibility for the payment (Ridley, 2006). Although practitioners who contributed to the case studies expressed the view that this should not be an excluding condition, rather it should be ensured that adequate support is in place, it is easy to see how such a statement could make it appear that the policy was not suitable for large groups of community care recipients.

As stated, older people were initially excluded from the 1996 Act but were eventually permitted access from 2000. Despite being the biggest group of service users (Clark, 2006), older people do not currently account for a large number of direct payments recipients, although numbers have increased steadily since the policy was extended to this group (see chapter 1). Clark (2006) found that direct payments were not introduced as a choice but rather were presented as a 'last resort' when it became apparent that provided services were not adequately meeting assessed needs. There are several reasons why practitioners might not consider direct payments when arranging services. As the policy was not originally available to this group it is possible that an information lag exists, resulting in take-up being behind that of groups who have been eligible since the enabling Act. It is also possible that older people, like those with learning difficulties and mental health problems, have been considered less likely to be able to cope with the responsibility of managing the payment and personal assistants. Therefore, it is not considered an option unless there is an obvious source of support, such as a family member. However, support from formal support organisations was also found to be important, although they too felt that older people required more support than younger disabled people (Clark, 2006).

Discussion in chapter 3 also highlighted the additional considerations around support as user groups diversify. As detailed, support organisations such as CILs have largely focused their services on those with physical impairments and might not always be able to provide appropriate support. One study involving mental health service users, for example, highlighted the importance of peer support from the support organisation (Ridley, 2006). Similarly, peer support for older people might not be available or easily accessible (Clark, 2006), whilst it might not be considered appropriate for those managing a direct payment on behalf of someone else to receive 'peer' support from a direct payments user.

Users' views from the case study authorities

The rest of this chapter will explore the impact of direct payments and personalisation of care from the user perspective. After explaining how information about users' views was collected, the discussion will explore issues around accessing information and how users became aware of direct payments in the local areas. This is followed by looking at issues around the management of the payment and how the local authority facilitates this process. Moving on from the broader focus on support organisations in chapter 3, user experiences of these organisations' roles are explored. Following on from this, broader debates around the transition to becoming an employer and negotiating relationships with personal assistants are considered. In highlighting this shift towards a more autonomous user identity, the chapter concludes by examining user views in relation to the 'ownership' of the direct payment.

Collecting information about users' views

In local authority 1 (see appendix 2), although users themselves were invited to participate in the focus groups, those who attended managed the payments on behalf of their adult children. Therefore it is not the direct voice of the user which is represented in discussion from this area. Two further interviews were completed with non-users – people who had decided not to proceed with the direct payment. The inclusion of these interviews highlights some of the barriers which have deterred some disabled people from taking on a direct payment.

In local authority 2 (see appendix 3), there were seven participants in the focus group. This included six users and the parent of a young disabled woman. In addition, three non-users participated.

The case studies aimed to elicit the views and experiences of a range of people using direct payments across all user groups, as well as service users who had chosen not to use a direct payment. However, we found that several groups were under-represented or not represented at all. In particular, the views of mental health service users were not well represented, whilst people with learning difficulties were represented by a family member who either helped them to manage the payment or received it in their own name on behalf of the disabled person.

Since legislation in 2003 made it mandatory to offer direct payments to those assessed as requiring a community care service, it could be expected that service users would feel more involved in the planning of their care irrespective of whether they choose direct payments or continue to use traditional services, because they are afforded a choice. However, findings from the case studies indicated that this is not always the result. Whilst for some disabled people using direct payments has been a positive choice it had frequently arisen from dissatisfaction with existing services. For others, direct payments had been presented as the only option, for example respondents in a rural area were unable to access any other services. Whilst conducting the focus groups and telephone interviews it became apparent that there were several factors that influenced how easily people felt they were able to manage their payments: in particular, the role of the support organisation, the named care manager and the monitoring procedures. These factors will be explored in the following sections.

Initial awareness

How users were introduced to direct payments varied considerably. Whilst several had taken part in pilot schemes run in local authority 2 in the late 1990s and one had used an indirect payment in the 1980s before moving onto direct payments, others had heard about them only when it became apparent that traditional services were not working for them. The most common source by which people had initially found out about the policy was from a social worker or care manager. However, in local authority 1 several users reported hearing about them after a presentation by the support organisation at a local group, whilst it was also reported that it was not uncommon to hear about them from peers, particularly in the case of parents of disabled children. Those who were told about the policy by a care manager or social worker reported that it had been presented as a 'last resort', because services either were not suitable or, in the case of more rural users, were simply not available through traditional routes. In one case, a daughter's increased care needs meant that she was no longer eligible for ILF as she would spend eight days out of fourteen in residential care, so the mother took on a direct payment to continue that level of personal support for her daughter despite being anxious about the paperwork involved. Another mother provided full-time support for her adult son as she felt the service they had been offered, a day centre, was not suitable: this was before she discovered the option of a direct payment. This option was therefore a great relief to her and her husband:

> we were just sorry that we hadn't known about it quicker because by the time we actually got it set up, we were both very stressed, you know, physically and mentally with caring. By the time it was set up, we had been two years caring 24/7 ... we were quite desperate. (parent, focus group, local authority 1)

In another case, one user, who managed the payment for her teenage son, reported being offered little option other than a direct payment:

> I was told that, quite bluntly, ... I should be having a direct payment ... that it would be too difficult for, you know, an organisation, that particular care organisation to be able to look at my needs and the complex package I had. (parent, focus group, local authority 1)

Despite the policy being presented in this way she was very happy with the outcome and hoped that it would allow her son greater independence as he grew up. However, this example highlights a broader trend in local authorities where direct payments are only offered for more complex packages and not as a mainstream option.

Others, who managed their own payments, felt that a direct payment was the only way they could receive an adequate service. So even in these cases, it did not seem to have been a 'real' choice but rather the only acceptable option. Respondents from both case study areas reported dissatisfaction with previous services provided by the local authorities and agencies. Although some examples of good practice were reported, many were not happy about the inconsistencies resulting from services being provided by a succession of different people. Indeed, several users indicated that if they could receive the same service without having the responsibility they would not take a direct payment. This view was particularly common among those who managed the payment on behalf of someone else.

Experiences of accessing the payments varied considerably in the two authorities. Whilst in local authority 1 those using direct payments reported that they had been able to access them fairly easily, users in local authority 2 reported lengthy waits, leading to feelings that social work staff were not keen for them to access the policy. However, several non-direct payments users interviewed in local authority 2 stated that they would have liked to take on a direct payment but that their applications had been delayed. One couple had requested a direct payment but were forced to rely on directly provided services following a dispute with the local authority about the size of package they would receive. Although it had been agreed that they could have a direct payment they had been placed on a waiting list as the designated budget had been spent.

Managing the payment and local authority monitoring

Discussion in earlier chapters has indicated that the monitoring of direct payments and the increased workload associated with it for practitioners was a key concern. In local authority 1, the support organisation was likely to take over these roles, whereas in local authority 2, this remained an ongoing concern for social work staff. Similarly most of the users across both areas reported that the financial management of the payment was indeed one of the main disadvantages of using a direct payment. In particular, respondents reported feeling anxious about the financial monitoring of the payment by the local authority. Reasons for this anxiety varied. Whilst some were very aware that the payment was not 'their' money, others felt that the monitoring systems were intrusive, overly bureaucratic and complex. Users were required to have the direct payment paid into a separate bank account. However, in local authority 2, it was felt that the reason for this had not been adequately explained and it was interpreted as being another barrier that had been put in the way. Further, a lack of information about the monitoring requirements, such as whether users should keep photocopies of everything submitted, created more anxiety. The role of the support organisation in assisting users with monitoring forms and providing a payroll service was therefore found to be very important and is discussed further below.

Supporting roles: users' views

As detailed in chapter 3, the models of support varied between the local authorities. Local authority 1 had a designated user-led service developed specifically for direct payments, whilst in local authority 2 this role was organised through the local CIL. Support was seen as an important component in managing the payment, and several respondents thought it was vital if the payment was to be successful. One respondent, who managed a payment for her son, commented:

> I think you need support from your social worker and you need support from [the support organisation] and you need support from everybody that you're working with because you're actually providing a service and I think you should be supported in providing that service. (parent, focus group, local authority 1)

Almost all respondents interviewed used the local support organisation for advice and information and a majority used its payroll services. However, the level and type of support offered differed across the local authorities. In local authority 1, the more rural area, support focused on direct payments and the organisation did not have the wider remit of independent living encompassed by the CIL in local authority 2. The organisation offered fairly intensive support and, in part due to the rural nature of the area, often visited its clients. However, despite this organisation offering a higher level of support, respondents still reported that they would like more input and were particularly keen that they should be able to get hold of someone on the telephone at short notice. Further, support needs were ongoing and in both areas users expressed a wish for support with the local authority monitoring procedures and recruitment of personal assistants.

The payroll service seemed to be the most frequently used service, with most respondents indicating that they felt that it allowed them to use the payment without becoming bogged down in the administrative aspects of it. Whilst some users were not concerned about running a payroll, others, across both areas, reported feeling intimidated by the fact that they would be responsible for ensuring tax and national insurance contributions were correctly met. This was identified as one of the disadvantages of using a direct payment and was frequently cited as an initial anxiety when people were considering using a direct payment. For some, however, having the payroll managed by the support organisation meant that they were confident and willing to take on the payment.

Users from both areas welcomed the fact that the support organisations were independent of social services. Indeed, in both areas respondents appeared to feel more confident asking for advice from the organisation than from their care manager. Whilst social workers acted as gatekeepers to services, users could ask support organisations about ways the policy can be used without fearing it might affect their service provision. Further, respondents, anxious to use the policy 'correctly', largely regarded support organisations as being experts in direct payments and so were likely to contact them for advice. For example, one user in local authority 1 commented that, when experiencing a problem:

I wouldn't have even tried to contact my social worker. (parent of
user, focus group, local authority 1)

Both support organisations offered support and advice in all areas of
recruiting personal assistants, including writing a job description, interviewing
and drafting contracts. As they were involved in the administrative aspects
of using the policy it is perhaps not surprising that they were also seen as an
accessible source of more general information.

Support from social workers varied. Some users were angered by their
social worker's apparent lack of knowledge about direct payments. Indeed,
several users reported receiving very little support from practitioners, most
notably in local authority 2. This lack of support left them feeling that the
policy did not have the backing of the local authority, leading one respondent
to comment:

I think [the] social work department wants direct payments to fail.
(user, focus group, local authority 2)

Information

Respondents in both areas indicated that, at times, they would have liked
more information regarding their package. This normally related to what
the payment could be used for. Many respondents reported feeling great
responsibility for how the payment was used and thus it was important
that they had access to reliable information. This seemed to be a particular
problem in local authority 2, where several respondents reported that they
had little confidence in the information they had been given by social work
staff:

we're all getting the different stories, I don't really, you know
nobody seems to be giving us the kind of right information (user,
focus group, local authority 2)

Another stated:

I was frightened to use [the direct payment] in case I went over the
mark ... I was told [by the care manager] that if the money built up,
you could use it for a holiday or respite but then somebody else told
me that you can't (user, focus group, local authority 2)

Although some users in the same area reported that they used the payment
as they felt appropriate and took the view that their social worker would let
them know should they be doing so incorrectly, for others it clearly led to
anxiety and users did not get the full benefit of using the payment.

Whilst respondents in local authority 1 had some concerns about how the payment could be used, the close relationship between the support organisation and the users meant that they felt they had greater opportunities to access information.

For many users it was important to be able to speak to an adviser, from either the support organisation or the local authority. Indeed, written materials, where available, were considered to be unhelpful as an alternative to one-to-one contact. For example, one user in local authority 1 felt that if she was already stressed because of caring for her son, if she had a problem with the payment she would not be able to sit and read a manual, and even if she could she would need support to act upon it.

It seemed that although users liked to know they had ongoing access to support, their main need for information was concentrated around the period in which they were deciding whether or not to use a direct payment and the start-up period. Indeed, several users reported that once the payment was up and running they had little need for contact with social work unless they had a specific query.

Recruitment and relationship with personal assistants

For most respondents across the two areas, being able to choose their own personal assistants was the biggest benefit of using a direct payment. This was particularly prevalent among those parents in local authority 1 who managed payments on behalf of their children (both adult and under 18). As one commented:

> It makes it all worthwhile, why you go through this [the practical management of the payment], because you get to choose all the carers. (parent of user, focus group, local authority 1)

Others who employed their own personal assistants appreciated the control being an employer gave them and this, for many, outweighed the difficulties of recruitment some had encountered. Employing staff allowed users to find people they felt were appropriate to work with them or their family member. For example, the parent of a user in local authority 2 felt that it was important that their daughter's personal assistants should be of similar age so that they could undertake age-appropriate activities and offer peer support as well as 'care'. Users also felt that employing people directly offered more control than employing agency staff, although it was felt that using agency staff was preferable to using directly provided services. Further, as they were able to arrange services in the way that suited them, direct payments users felt they could get the best value from their package.

Some respondents had used the same personal assistants for many years: for example, one user who was no longer eligible for ILF continued to employ her personal assistant with a direct payment instead. However, others, particularly those with larger packages, reported finding recruitment difficult, although in all areas users thought that the assistance from the support organisations was particularly helpful.

As support was often personal and delivered within the home it was sometimes unsettling for users, who felt that privacy was lost and their autonomy within their own home undermined. Parents who managed payments on behalf of their children, both adult and under 18, reported that having to open their homes to a variety of people was not easy, but that employing people with a direct payment went some way to redressing the power balance within the home. The benefits in terms of providing a personalised service made it worthwhile. As one woman commented:

> I mean, it's not easy. There's no way you can say that it's easy having people in and out of your home, sleeping in your home overnight, you know, coming in at ten o'clock ... but I've accepted that if my son was going to have an independent life away from us and really helping his normal development as much as I could that was the price we must pay; to lose our privacy, if you like. (parent of user, focus group, local authority 1)

The intimate nature of the roles undertaken by many of the personal assistants caused some difficulties when boundaries became blurred. Personal assistants were required to work closely with families and individuals and close relationships sometimes evolved. For some parents who had employed personal assistants to work with their children it was important to feel that the employee cared for their son or daughter on a personal as well as professional level. However, this made it difficult for some respondents to regard the relationship as purely professional. For example, when one respondent's son's personal assistant became ill with stress and decided to leave her job, the mother found it particularly distressing as she felt she had been let down personally as well as professionally:

> this was somebody that had been with us for 14 months and swore allegiance to [my son] and, you know, totally committed and, I mean, she was a good carer, a really good carer ... Loved [my son] to bits and [he] loved her. (parent of user, focus group, local authority 1)

Others acknowledged that it could be a difficult relationship for the personal assistants:

> it's difficult for the carers to come to you to say to complain about your son, if you like. Or to complain about the conditions or to ask you things because ... they see you as the parent first. (parent of user, focus group, local authority 1)

This was not only the case for those who managed payments on behalf of others. For example, users in local authority 2 were able to access training to be an employer through the support organisation and thought this was useful, not only in terms of providing information about their requirements, but also to help them gain confidence. Users recognised that it was important to build good relationships with staff, although this required considerable input from the employer. For those who lacked confidence or access to good support, managing personal assistants could be harder, as demonstrated by one user in local authority 2 whose anxiety about losing her personal assistant allowed the employee to dictate the terms on which she would work.

Retention of personal assistants was a concern and had been a problem for some users. Several were well aware that it was not a well-paid job and, for some workers, was not an attractive long-term career prospect. Users in local authority 1 thought that this could be overcome if personal assistants were able to undertake SVQs or other means of continuing professional development. Users in local authority 2 also commented that it was difficult to expect professional care if personal assistants' wages were so low. They were particularly frustrated that agencies were paid considerably more to provide carers than they were given to employ personal assistants. Indeed, half the group had found that the rate offered was too low to attract appropriate staff. This is perhaps particularly likely to be a problem in a large urban area such as this, where there are many employment opportunities and direct payments users cannot rely as much on being able to employ personal assistants already known to them, as users in rural areas seemed able to do.

'Ownership' of the direct payment

Perhaps one of the biggest contrasts between the respondents from the two areas was that those who took part from local authority 1, the more rural area, managed payments on behalf of someone else, most commonly an adult child. As indicated, users managing a payment on behalf of someone else took part in all focus groups but, despite invitations to a wider range of participants, nobody managing their own payment participated in a focus group or interview in local authority 1. Both practitioners and a support organisation representative reported that this was not surprising: much of the direct payments promotion was aimed at carers' organisations and, although the support organisation was user-led, there was no organisation of disabled people in the area. Thus the respondents' views about the purposes of the policy varied from those of users who managed payments for themselves (local authority 2), to those who were acting on behalf of their children. In these cases, policy was seen as a solution for the whole family, for example to reduce the level of support they provided, rather than as a means of enabling increased independence. In the case of one respondent there was some conflict about who decided what the personal assistants did. The respondent's son lived in his own flat and was the formal manager of the payment, with the support of his mother. However, his mother felt that he was not capable of deciding what he wanted to do on a daily basis and found it difficult to balance his role as the employer and her role in helping him manage the payment:

> it's a difficult position for us because we're saying to the carers 'right, get back to us, check with us [before doing something] rather than land yourself in trouble', so it's difficult, it's quite stressful. (parent of user, focus group, local authority 1)

She acknowledged that this also made the situation awkward for the personal assistants:

> it's quite difficult sometimes because, if you like, he's the name that's on top of the payslip and he's the employer, but with our support. So he can appear quite well sometimes and say to the carers 'don't do this and don't do that, take me here or take me there or go home early or stay late' ... and it's difficult for the carer because you know, he's the employer yet I'm the employer 'cos I'm the one that's doing the timesheets and I'm the one that does the staff meetings. (parent of user, focus group, local authority 1)

These comments clearly raise issues around ownership of the payment and the broad purpose of the policy. In this instance it could be interpreted that the direct payment allowed the mother to maintain control over her son's activities. Indeed, in another case the respondent consistently referred to the payment as her own, although it was provided to meet her son's assessed needs. There was a considerable focus on meeting personal care requirements, and the idea of the payment increasing the autonomy of the disabled person was not really considered. Although one user said that it would enable her son to receive a personalised service and live more independently, she intended this to take place within the family home and according to her wishes.

Conclusion

There were many common themes among the users' experiences, running across both case study areas. It was apparent that, although users' support requirements and expectations of what the support organisation should provide varied, it was important to all user groups that ongoing support was available. For the main part, users seemed to prefer that this support came from support organisations which they regarded as the 'experts' in direct payments. Indeed, preference for user-led support underlines broader findings from users across the UK, in both the ESRC study and wider research (see Barnes and Mercer, 2006). This was associated with the lack of confidence in the knowledge of social workers expressed by some users in both case study areas, which in some cases had led users to feel alienated from the social work department. However, when practitioners worked in conjunction with the support organisation, they were perceived as being more supportive even if they were not thought to be knowledgeable. Ability to manage the financial aspects of payment, and in particular the completion of the required monitoring arrangements, had been a major concern of users across the two areas, both before they undertook the payment and whilst it was underway. Again, when looking at these concerns, it was apparent that the role of the support organisation was important. Users required both practical help to complete forms and support to learn to manage it themselves. The necessity of having access to information about how the payment can be used was also frequently raised by respondents, who felt that they were unable to make full use of it, as they were concerned about misspending the money.

The perceived purpose of using a direct payment differed among users. Many of those who managed their own payments were aware of the independent living movement and spoke of the control and choice the policy offered them as a means to achieve greater independence. However, for other respondents, particularly those who managed, or helped manage, a direct payment for someone else, the policy was often presented as a last resort when directly provided services were not available or were not considered suitable. Thus the payment was as much about fulfilling the needs of the family member as those of the disabled person. As well as potentially causing conflicts over ownership, this represents a shift in policy and moves it away from the aim of independent living. Whilst shared management allows direct payments to become available to people who would not otherwise be able to access them, it might also in some cases mean that control simply shifts from the local authority to the person providing support, without taking into account the wishes of the disabled person.

However, regardless of who managed the payment, all respondents spoke of the opportunity that direct payments offered for personalised support and the benefits of being able to exercise choice and control were widely recognised. All respondents recognised the benefits offered by person-centred care in terms of health and well-being as well as wider life. Respondents also welcomed the change in role they took on by employing personal assistants, whether it was to provide support for them or for someone else, despite the management this involved. Although several participants would rather not have had to manage the financial side of the payment, this was outweighed by the autonomy it offered.

CHAPTER 6

The Future of Direct Payments in Scotland

Charlotte Pearson

Introduction

This final chapter brings together the key themes set out in this book. In doing this, discussion moves on to explore some of the potential future pathways for direct payments in Scotland. Discussion highlights how the original market and independent living policy discourses underpinning direct payments have been reconceptualised and developed through New Labour's policy agenda. However, these themes are shown to have been used in different ways north and south of the border.

Overview of themes in the book

Throughout this book, discussion has outlined how local authorities, Holyrood and central government administrations have responded to direct payments in Scotland over the past decade. Whilst there has been a rapid expansion in take-up over the last five years, there are proportionately only half as many users as in England, with significant geographical inequities both within Scotland and across the UK. Findings from the telephone interviews and case studies highlighted some of the broader problems in terms of the structuring of policy. It has become clear that overall services have not been reorganised to enable increased payment access, and in the example of local authority 2 a separate cash-limited budget has been established for the policy. As discussion in chapter 5 showed, this has resulted in a waiting list and substantial delays for potential users. Direct payments therefore remain a marginal service option, with most local authorities reluctant to promote the policy as a mainstream alternative to directly provided services, at least in the immediate future.

Our findings from users showed a general enthusiasm for direct payments but there were frustrations around their organisation across all case study areas – from initial access to their accountability once in place. Indeed, there remain problems with some social work staff. As indicated in chapters 2, 4 and elsewhere (see Stainton, 2002), the role of social workers is critical in terms of facilitating access to the direct payment. Whilst in some cases these may be viewed positively, there remain problems in terms of practitioner knowledge and enthusiasm about direct payments. In turn, the policy is still seen by many as a form of 'backdoor privatisation' (Pearson, 2004a) – a view not helped by the negative attitudes of trade unions in some areas. As our findings showed, these clearly impacted on users' experiences. Also important are issues around the perceived purpose of direct payments. Notably the absence of actual users participating in the focus groups in local authority 1 highlighted broader concerns over the ownership of direct payments, which positioned the policy as a 'last resort' where more traditional care packages had failed. These examples once again push the policy away from the ethos of independent living and towards a more restricted system of personalised care.

Users' accounts in both case study areas did, however, underline the importance of supporting roles in facilitating their payment packages. In particular, local authority organisation of these responsibilities has raised broader questions around the role of support organisations and the future of user-led services. As Barnes and Mercer (2006) observe, many local authorities and professionals have been less than impressed by the user-led philosophy and view it simply as a different way of delivering a broadly similar set of health and social services. Likewise, as chapter 4 highlighted, the association of direct payments with a developing care market has in many ways overshadowed the origins of the policy as a means of enabling independent living and thereby empowering disabled people. For user-led organisations like the CILs, whilst direct payments have presented them with an opportunity to formalise their expertise and secure the appropriate funding to facilitate this, they have increasingly found themselves competing for restrictive contracts which may undermine broader areas of their work. As the case study examples reported in chapter 3 illustrate, the designated user-led direct payments support service in local authority 1 had been allocated a far wider remit of tasks related to the policy than the CIL in local authority 2. This clearly reflects a number of factors and it is important to take into account local political cultures. However, any resistance to incorporating wider CIL roles into campaigning and service provision around independent living clearly impacts on their capacity to challenge the existing network of support for disabled people. It is also important to note that local authorities in Scotland have received significantly less additional money to develop support roles than their counterparts in England, and this has clearly limited their capacity to develop support strategies. Likewise, as discussion in the next section indicates, the role of local CILs has been promoted in more recent policy documents as part of a broader strategy to draw on the direct payments model through the personalisation of care and promotion of user-led services. However, as commentary will show, indications so far show a clear lead on this from England, with a more muted response from the Scottish Executive.

Developing the direct payments model: re-launching familiar discourses?

Over the past few years, New Labour has clearly set out its support for the ethos of direct payments as a model of service provision and, as specified earlier in the book, has promoted them as an integral part of its modernisation agenda within social care. However, when looking at the detail of policy discussion so far, it is only possible to link this to a broadly English agenda, with a far more limited commentary emerging from the Scottish Executive.

Indeed, English support for direct payments was clearly set out in 2003 by the then Community Care Minister, Stephen Ladyman, in advocating that:

> The assumption should be not only will care be delivered by a direct payment; the assumption should be that the person can manage a direct payment and the only times when care should be delivered, in my view, other than by a direct payment, is when the individual themselves has made a personal and positive choice to receive the care directly and not via a direct payment. (NCIL, 2003)

In stating this, Ladyman clearly envisaged direct payments as the mainstream option within community care services. Whilst the Scottish Ministers have articulated a broad commitment to the policy (see Brankin, 2005 in Scottish Parliament, 2005b) and some additional monies have been made available to local authorities from 2006 to enable increased take-up (DPS News, 2005), no similar statement of support has been publicly made. Therefore in order to assess the future of direct payments in Scotland in more detail, it is necessary to examine the broader policy context and developments in this area.

Since mandatory implementation of direct payments in 2003, several key policy documents have been published which impact on their future direction. As discussion in this section details, in many ways the ideas presented in these documents revisit the key strands of policy. On the one hand, some of the recent policy documents have linked in with an independent living discourse through pledges to reconfigure the wider network of support for disabled people. At the same time, direct payments remain lodged within a broader welfare market agenda, with this rhetoric reconstructed around a new focus on the 'personalisation of care'.

Central to New Labour's modernisation agenda within social care and health has been an emphasis on 'partnerships' between different provider agencies (Glendinning, Powell and Rummery, 2002). As Barnes and Mercer (2006) note, these can take on a number of forms but centre on joint working relationships which may involve links between private, voluntary and public sectors. At the same time, policy change within social care and health has incorporated a focus on the notion of enhanced personalisation of services.

Notably, publication of the pamphlet *Personalisation through Participation* (Leadbeater, 2004) by Demos encapsulated New Labour's enthusiasm for this concept:

> Personalisation is a very potent but highly contested and ambiguous idea that could be as influential as privatisation was in the 1980s and 1990s in reshaping public provision ... (Leadbeater, 2004: 18)

Leadbeater (2004) argues that personalised public services could have at least five different meanings – many of which may be operationalised through direct payments. Firstly, this is linked to the provision of a 'more customer-friendly interface with existing services' (Leadbeater, 2004: 21). This relates to clearer access to services around user needs. Secondly, he argues that once access has been secured, users should have clearer options and choices within services. Thirdly, personalisation is related to giving users an increased say over how money is spent and thereby more power to make decisions about their service needs. This links to the fourth area, which emphasises the roles of users as not only service consumers, but co-designers and producers of services. In turn, the fifth meaning links practice into a more collectivised response through a push towards self-organisation of services.

This framework of service organisation clearly revisits a number of themes around consumerism and empowerment which were set out during the early 1990s, particularly through the 1990 NHS and Community Care Act. Moreover, their broad emphasis on 'voice' and 'exit' strategies of empowerment draw on earlier conceptualisations of empowerment in the public services by Hirschman (1970). However this renewed focus on 'personalisation' by New Labour does present a number of opportunities for developing the direct payments model as discussion in several key policy documents has indicated.

Developing a focus on independent living: an English agenda?

In terms of looking at the broader reorganisation of service provision for disabled people, the publication *Improving the Life Chances of Disabled People* (ILCDP) (Prime Minister's Strategy Unit et al., 2005) drew strongly on the rhetoric of both partnership and personalisation and highlighted the direct payments model as a means of facilitating an independent living agenda.

ILCDP sets out a comprehensive strategy to transform the structure of services and support for disabled people of working age, disabled children and their families and promises that by 2025 'disabled people should have full opportunities and choices to improve their quality of life and be respected and included as equal members of society' (Prime Minister's Strategy Unit et al., 2005: 4). Rather than restricting reform to discrete policy areas, its strength lies in its definition of independent living. This acknowledged the need to focus reform across the key policy areas of social care, health, housing, transport and education.

Overall, ILCDP was well received by the disability movement in the UK. Its development drew on extensive research and consultation with a variety of stakeholders, including disabled people and disabled representatives of organisations (Barnes and Mercer, 2006), and its policy development is based on a social model analysis of disability. Indeed, BCODP described it as 'one of the most positive documents to come from government, relating to disabled people, in many years' (BCODP, 2005: 1).

When looking at the development of the direct payments model through ILCDP, two key areas can be identified. The first is through a call to extend different approaches to direct payments to disabled people through 'individualised budgets'. Lack of coherence and poor access to support and services for disabled people has long been criticised (see, for example, Berthoud, 1993). Therefore, it is envisaged that a shift to an individualised and unified budget should encourage greater flexibility, freedom and choice and move away from the current fragmentation of service provision for disabled people across national and local tiers of government.

As Barnes and Mercer (2006) explain, individualised budgets would enable independent living by bringing together the various sources of support. This unified budget would be based on assessed need, with the individual service user deciding how to use the allocated money. This could be used along the same lines as a direct payment, or alternatively as a mixture of services and cash payment.

The second area of interest for direct payments outlined in ILCDP was a pledge to establish a user-led CIL in every local authority by 2010. Leadbeater's focus on 'self-organising solutions' (Leadbeater, 2004: 22) clearly links with the broader personalisation agenda. Whilst ILCDP suggests that newly established CILs will need to adapt to local circumstances, a number of key areas of service development are listed. These include those which link in with the current support roles developed by many direct payments support organisations, such as information and advice; advocacy and peer support; assistance with self-assessment; support in using individual budgets; and support to recruit and employ personal assistants. However, this list is expanded to include broader tasks related to the promotion of independent living, such as disability equality training (Prime Minister's Strategy Unit et al., 2005: 77).

Discussion in chapter 3 highlighted some of the problems experienced by CILs in negotiating their roles as support organisation providers for direct payments users. This suggested that many local authorities have been reluctant to fund CIL work that extends beyond the remit of direct payments support. Therefore the proposed shift to a wider network of CILs may challenge this perception and open new opportunities for the user-led movement. However, as Barnes and Mercer (2006) caution, although this move may allow new funding streams to these organisations, the shift to this type of 'partnership' model could reduce autonomy and enhance regulation by central government.

More importantly from a Scottish perspective, despite the fact that some elements of ILCDP are matters for UK-wide application, such as benefit reform, the Executive has made no formal comment on how this and other proposals set out in ILCDP will be developed. Shortly after the report was published in February 2005, the then Minister for Communities, Malcolm Chisholm, answered a parliamentary question on whether the Scottish Executive would develop the recommendations set out in the report. He stated that, 'we note the UK Government's report with interest', but added that 'it has no specific recommendations for action by the Scottish Executive' (Scottish Parliament, 2005a).

Although the report does cover devolved areas including health and social care, the focus on restructuring support for disabled people through unified and individualised budgets links in with broader areas of social security. This also extends into areas of other forms of direct payments – notably the Independent Living Fund, Access to Work and the Disabled Facilities Grant. Indeed, the inclusion of the Department of Work and Pensions as a key author shows the need for policy development at a UK level. However, given the muted response from the Scottish Executive, this is evidently not clear within the context of the document. Other initiatives across the Executive such as Joint Future (Scottish Executive, 2000b), which promotes links between health, community and housing, and Supporting People (Scottish Executive, 2003b), which has integrated funding for housing support services, draw on models of individualised budgets. The absence of a response to ILCDP from the Scottish Executive, and the lack of clarity from Westminster over this, therefore impacts on progress from both tiers of government.

In contrast, a series of initiatives have been developed in England which draw on themes around direct payments, personalisation and independent living. Following on from ILCDP, the Department of Health (DoH) published the Green Paper *Independence, Well-being and Choice* (DoH, 2005) in March 2005. This also pursued the theme of individualised budgets and set out how these would be organised through health and social care (Glasby, Glendinning and Littlechild, 2006). More recently, this support has been echoed in the White Paper *Our Health, Our Care, Our Say* (DoH, 2006). Whilst both papers emphasise the need to encourage the take-up of direct payments among key groups such as older people, people with mental health problems and young disabled people in transition, Barnes and Mercer (2006) (writing about the Green Paper), argue that there are relatively few innovative policy suggestions. Unlike ILCDP, both papers remain lodged in the language of 'care', make no mention of a social model analysis of disability and offer no definition of independent living. However, Glasby, Glendinning and Littlechild (2006) suggest that recent policy initiatives are significant for the future of direct payments in that they have pushed them into the mainstream of public policy in England. But there remain questions as to whether a similar line will be pursued in Scotland.

As suggested, Barnes and Mercer's critique of the DoH's approach to direct payments centres on the positioning of direct payments as a means to facilitate 'care' for disabled people. This underlines ongoing concerns – and those illustrated through some of the users' experiences set out in chapter 5 – that direct payments are being used as part of a cash-limited social care market, rather than a means to facilitate independent living (see also Pearson, 2000). ILCDP is therefore clearly important because it acknowledges the need for full-scale reform of services for disabled people and for including a working definition of independent living at the heart of this. Indeed, this has been developed through proposals set out in the Independent Living (Disabled Persons) Bill, which at the time of writing was expected to receive its first reading in May 2006.

The Independent Living Bill has been developed by Lord Ashley in consultation with the Disability Rights Commission (DRC). Overall it sets out a framework of principles for the delivery of social care. This centres on the provision of 'empowering and culturally sensitive support for participation and equal citizenship' (DRC, 2006). Given the main focus on social care and health legislation, the bill primarily covers England and Wales, although like ILCDP the wider implications of reform impact on policy throughout the UK.

Drawing on areas covered by ILCDP, the bill aims to provide the necessary legislative framework to facilitate independent living. In its briefing on the bill, the DRC highlights the importance of direct payments in doing this, and emphasises the need to target groups with lower take-up (DRC, 2006: paragraph 4.8). Similarly, the focus on individualised budgets is underlined as a means to unify existing funding streams for disabled people (paragraph 4.9). Again, this is underpinned by the promotion of user-led support services such as CILs (paragraph 4.13).

What's the future for direct payments in Scotland?

In chapter 1, it was suggested that policy development for direct payments has tended to follow in the same direction as England, but at a more cautious rate. However, as discussion so far has shown, over the past year (2005-06) the focus on developing the direct payments model in England has gained momentum. This has been achieved through its links with a broader theme of personalisation within social care and health – notably through individualised budgets – and a higher profile recognition of independent living, initially through ILCDP and now through the Independent Living (Disabled Persons)

Bill. The outcome of these changes still remains to be seen – given the long passage required to secure direct payments on the statute book (see Glasby and Littlechild, 2002), any progress is likely to be slow. However, these important changes have placed a divide between policy development north and south of the border.

As suggested, the heightened profile of direct payments across recent policy documents in England have yet to receive the same impetus in Scotland. Although the rhetoric of personalisation has featured in a number of key documents, critically this has not been specifically linked to an independent living agenda. For example, *Changing Lives: Report of the 21st Century Social Work Review* stated that it would 'challenge the way that we organise both social work and other public services and call for new roles for workers' (Scottish Executive, 2006: 3). However, very little detail is given in terms of how direct payments might fit into a broader reorganisation of services, with discussion limited to the ethos of their role. As noted in chapter 4, the shift to mandatory implementation of direct payments in 2003 presented policy as a 'new initiative' in many local authorities, despite their availability since 1997. A similar sentiment is indeed reiterated in the Social Work Review:

> The introduction of direct payments is the beginning of a move towards people having more purchasing power. People will increasingly expect to determine the services they will use, be they delivered by public, private or voluntary sector organisations or by directly employing their own care staff. (Scottish Executive, 2006: 3)

Direct payments have also featured in Scottish health initiatives – again linking in with the broader personalisation agenda. In the White Paper *Delivering for Health* (Scottish Executive, 2005b), increasing the uptake of direct payments is cited as a means of providing better support for people with long-term conditions and of avoiding more complex service responses, but little more detail is given.

Overall, there lacks a cohesion on direct payments across Scottish government departments to develop policy within a broader framework of independent living. Moves by the Executive to promote take-up in local authorities have, however, emerged more recently. As stated in chapter 3, the allocation of £1.8 million in 2006-07 and £2 million the following year (DPS News, 2005) to develop support organisations and designated direct payments posts in areas where these have not been forthcoming demonstrates a commitment to future development. Furthermore, additional grants have been made available to different interest groups involved in promoting direct payments support roles. These include payments of £35,000 for the three-year period between 2006 and 2009 to a consortium of Scottish direct payments support organisations to develop the work previously carried out by DPS on providing information support to its members. The CILs and their partners have also received targeted investment of £70,000 for 2006–09 to facilitate support training, and funds allocated to SPAEN (£50,000 in 2006-07, £70,000 for 2007 and £70,000 for 2008) will facilitate awareness training on direct payments, mainly for those considering becoming a personal assistance employer. Support roles will also be diversified through the allocation of monies to develop more specialist training for disabled children service users and mental health service users. Yet there remain gaps in pursuing the broader ethos of direct payments as part of a broader reorganisation of services for disabled people.

Conclusions

Discussion throughout this book has set out the position of direct payments in Scotland as implementation of the Act nears its tenth anniversary. Although progress has been made during this time which has seen a significant number of disabled people gain access to direct payments, their experiences remain marginal in the overall provision of support. There are some grounds for optimism, as initiatives announced since 2005 have sought to raise the profile of direct payments. However, any change will require a broader focus, not only on the benefits of direct payments, but on how these can be integrated into a more widespread agenda for independent living.

Background to the ESRC study

The ESRC study was set up to examine the key differences in direct payments policies, implementation strategies and practices in Scotland, England, Wales and Northern Ireland. This focused on the experiences of policy planners and practitioners in terms of how policy impacted on broader patterns of welfare provision, as well as looking at their impact on disabled people in different parts of the UK.

Data collection was organised through three key stages. The first stage included a review of policy development and statistical analysis of reported figures (see Riddell et al., 2005). Discussion at this stage was also supported by a series of interviews with key informants from across the UK. Those involved were selected on the basis of their knowledge or expertise in relation to direct payments, including representatives of disability organisations; local authorities; central government and its devolved regions; and key activists involved in the early development of direct payments practice and policy. Stage 2 centred on a series of telephone interviews with leading direct payments personnel across local authorities (and HSS in Northern Ireland). In Scotland, interviews covered 30 out of the 32 local authorities and were conducted between November 2004 and April 2005. The interviews were semi-structured and covered a range of issues including the development of direct payments policy; the impact of guidance from central government or devolved administrations; the capacity and demand for direct payments from different user groups; the role of support organisations; the use of direct payments and a focus on labour market conditions. Interviews lasted between 25 and 60 minutes and (in all but two cases) were recorded and transcribed. Transcripts were coded using key themes from the interview schedule.

The third stage of the research focused on case studies of policies, practices and procedures in eight local areas – two from each part of the UK (see chapter 2 for details of the Scottish examples). Case study local authorities were chosen for a number of reasons. These included urban-rural locality, socio-economic mix, level of resistance to direct payments (this was explored in the telephone interviews) and the extent to which research had previously been carried out in the area. Focus groups and semi-structured interviews were carried out with senior planning staff and frontline practitioners in each authority. This was followed by a series of focus groups with users and, where possible, interviews with people who had decided not to take on a direct payment.

Conduct of the local authority 1 case study

Interviews were conducted with the following individuals and groups in Autumn 2005. Two researchers were present at each focus group and a representative from the support organisation also attended the users focus group.

Focus group/interview	Participants
Focus group	6 social workers/care managers, finance officer
Telephone interview	1 social worker, learning difficulty team
Focus group	3 direct payment users
(Telephone) interview	2 direct payment users
Interview	2 non-direct payment users
Telephone interview	manager of support organisation
Telephone interview	Head of Social Services
Telephone interview	lead direct payments practitioner

The focus groups and telephone interviews covered a range of themes which were explored throughout the book. These included issues around training and information for users; accountability and monitoring; the relationship of direct payments to core services; user groups for which policy works best; the current status of direct payments in the local authority; recruitment and labour market issues; and the use of direct payments. As discussion shows, these themes were explored throughout the different interest groups and are documented accordingly.

APPENDIX 3

Conduct of the local authority 2 case study

Interviews were conducted with the following individuals and groups between Autumn 2005 and Spring 2006.

Focus group/interview	Participants
Focus group	6 social workers/care managers
Telephone interview	1 social worker, mental health team
Telephone interview	1 practice team leader, children and families team
Interview	1 direct payment user
Focus group	7 direct payment users
Focus group	3 non-direct payment users
Telephone interview	support organisation worker
Telephone interview	area team manager and community care representative on the Direct Payments Strategy Group
Telephone interview	1 Principal Finance Officer
Telephone interview	lead direct payments practitioner
Telephone interview	union representative

As detailed in appendix 1, a number of themes were explored with each group during interviews and focus groups and these are detailed throughout the book.

References

Barnes, C. and Mercer, G. (2006) *Independent Futures: Creating User-Led Disability Services in a Disabling Society*, Bristol: Policy Press

Berthoud, R., Lakey, J. and McKay, S. (1993) *The Economic Problems of Disabled People*, London: Policy Studies Institute

British Council of Disabled People (2005) *'Improving the Life Chances of Disabled People': a response from the British Council of Disabled People*. Available from URL: www.bcodp.org.uk/library/BCODP%20response%20to%20Improving%20Life%20Chances.doc (accessed April 2006)

Clark, H. (2006) '"It's meant that, well, I'm living a life now": older people's experience of direct payments', in Leece, J. and Bornat, J. (eds) (2006) *Developments in Direct Payments*, Bristol: Policy Press

Clark, H., Gough, H. and MacFarlane, A. (2004) *'It Pays Dividends': Direct Payments and Older People*, Bristol: Policy Press in association with Joseph Rowntree Foundation

Clarke, J., Gewirtz, S. and McLaughlin, E. (2000) *New Managerialism, New Welfare*, London: Sage

d' Aboville, E. (2006) 'Implementing direct payments: a support organisation perspective', in Leece, J. and Bornat, J. (eds) (2006) *Developments in Direct Payments*, Bristol: Policy Press

Department of Health (2005) *Independence, Well-being and Choice: Our Vision for the Future of Social Care for Adults in England*, Cm 6499, London: Department of Health

Department of Health (2006) *Our Health, Our Care, Our Say: A New Direction for Community Services*, Cm 6737, London: Department of Health

Direct Payments Scotland (2002) *Five Steps: A Guide for Local Authorities Implementing Direct Payments*. Edinburgh: Direct Payments Scotland

Direct Payments Scotland (2005) 'Direct payment support spreads throughout Scotland', DP News, September 2005. Available from URL: http://www.dpscotland.org.uk/0304dps/canedit/newsletters/NewsletterSept2005.asp (accessed May 2006)

Disability Rights Commission (2006) 'Briefing on Lord Ashley's Independent Living Bill. Available from URL: www.drc.org.uk/disabilitydebate/priorities/documents/briefing_on_il.doc (accessed July 2006)

DP News (2005) 'Executive announce extra funding to support direct payments', DP News, February

Evans, J. and Hasler, F. (1996) 'Direct payments campaign in the UK', presentation for the European Network on Independent Living Seminar, Stockholm: 9–11 June

Glasby, J. and Littlechild, R. (2002) *Social Work and Direct Payments*, Bristol: Policy Press

Glasby, J., Glendinning, C. and Littlechild, R. (2006) 'The future of direct payments', in Leece, J. and Bornat, J. (eds) (2006) *Developments in Direct Payments*, Bristol: Policy Press

Glendinning, C. (1992) 'Residualism versus rights: social policy and disabled people', in Manning, N. and Page, R. (eds) (1992) *Social Policy Review 4*, Canterbury: Social Policy Association

Glendinning, C., Powell, M. and Rummery, K. (2002) *Partnerships, New Labour and the Governance of Welfare*, Bristol: Policy Press

Gramlich, S., McBride, G., and Snelham, N. with Williams, V. and Simons, K. (2002) *Journey to Independence: How to Run Your Life with Direct Payments*, Kidderminster: BILD

Hasler, F. (2006) 'The Direct Payments Development Fund', in Leece, J. and Bornat, J. (eds) (2006) *Developments in Direct Payments*, Bristol: Policy Press

Hasler, F., Campbell, J. and Zarb, G. (1999) *Direct Routes to Independence: A Guide to Local Authority Implementation of Direct Payments*, London: PSI/NCIL

Hirschman, A. (1970) *Exit, Voice and Loyalty: Responses to Decline in Firms, Organisations and States*, Harvard: Harvard University Press

Kestenbaum, A. (1992) *Cash for Care: The Experience of Independent Living Clients*, Nottingham: Independent Living Fund

Kestenbaum, A. (1995) *An Opportunity Lost? Social Services Use of the Independent Living Transfer*, London: Disability Income Group

Leadbeater, C. (2004) *Personalisation through Participation: A New Script for Public Services*, London: Demos

Lipsky, M. (1980) *Street-level Bureaucracy: Dilemmas of the Individual in Public Services*, New York: Russell Sage Foundation

National Centre for Independent Living (2003) Transcript of speech by Stephen Ladyman, Parliamentary Under-Secretary of State, Department of Health, at National Centre for Independent Living launch event, 30 October 2003. Available from URL: www.ncil.org.uk/Stephen_LadymanNCILLaunch.asp (accessed April 2006)

Pearson, C. (2000) 'Money talks? Competing discourses in the implementation of direct payments', *Critical Social Policy*, Vol. 20, No. 4, pp. 459–77

Pearson, C. (2004a) 'Keeping the cash under control: What's the problem with direct payments in Scotland?', *Disability and Society*, Vol. 19 No. 1, pp. 3–14

Pearson, C. (2004b) 'The implementation of direct payments: issues for user-led organisations in Scotland', in Barnes, C. and Mercer, G. (eds) (2004) *Implementing the Social Model of Disability: Theory and Research*, Leeds: Disability Press

Pearson, C. (2006) 'Direct Payments in Scotland', in Leece, J. and Bornat, J. (eds) (2006) *Developments in Direct Payments*, Bristol: Policy Press

Priestley, M., Jolly, D., Pearson, C., Riddell, S., Barnes, C. and Mercer, G. (2006) 'Direct payments and disabled people in the UK: supply, demand and devolution' British Journal of Social Work, Advance Access published July 19 2006, 10.1093/bjsw/bcl063. Available from URL: http://bjsw.oxfordjournals.org

Prime Minister's Strategy Unit, Department of Work and Pensions, Department of Health, Department for Education and Skills, Office of the Deputy Prime Minister (2005) *Improving the Life Chances of Disabled People*, London: Cabinet Office, Prime Minister's Strategy Unit

Riddell, S., Pearson, C., Barnes, C., Jolly, D., Mercer, G. and Priestley, M. (2005) 'The development of direct payments in the UK: implications for social justice', *Social Policy and Society*, Vol. 4, No. 1, 75–85

Ridley, J. (2006) '"Direct what?" Exploring the suitability of direct payments for people with mental health problems', in Leece, J. and Bornat, J. (eds) (2006) *Developments in Direct Payments*, Bristol: Policy Press

Roll, J. (1996) *The Community Care (Direct Payments) Bill: Research Paper*, London: House of Commons Library

Scottish Executive (1999) *The Same As You? A Review of Services for People with Learning Difficulties*, Edinburgh: Scottish Executive

Scottish Executive (2000a) Community Care (Direct Payments) Act 1996: Community Care (Direct Payments) (Scotland) Amendment Regulations 2000, Circular No. CCD4/2000, Edinburgh: Scottish Executive

Scottish Executive (2000b) *Report of the Joint Future Group.* Available at URL: www. scotland.gov.uk (accessed May 2006)

Scottish Executive (2003a) *Social Work (Scotland) Act 1968: Sections 12B and C – Direct Payments: Policy and Practice Guidance.* Edinburgh: Scottish Executive Health Department, Community Care Division.

Scottish Executive (2003b) *Supporting People: Strategic Guidance and Interim Guidance.* Available from URL: www.scotland.gov.uk (accessed May 2006)

Scottish Executive (2005a) *Direct Payments Scotland 2005: Statistics Release.* Available at URL: www.scotland.gov.uk (accessed December 2005)

Scottish Executive (2005b) *Delivering for Health,* Edinburgh: Scottish Executive

Scottish Executive (2006) *Changing Lives: Report of the 21st Century Social Work Review,* Edinburgh: Scottish Executive

Scottish Office (1997) *Community Care (Direct Payments) Act 1996: Policy and Practice Guidance.* Enclosure to Circular No. SWSG3/97, Edinburgh: Scottish Office, Social Work Services Group

Scottish Parliament (2005a) Answer to written parliamentary question, 25 February 2005. Available at URL: www.scottish.parliament.uk/business/pqa/wa-05/wa0225.htm#20 (accessed May 2006)

Scottish Parliament (2005b) Answer to written parliamentary question, 3 March 2005. Available at URL: www.scottish.parliament.uk/business/pqa/wa-05/war0304.htm (accessed May 2006)

Stainton, T. (2002) 'Taking rights structurally: disability rights and social worker responses to direct payments', *British Journal of Social Work,* Vol. 32, pp. 751–63.

UNISON Scotland (2004) *Direct Payment Briefing.* Available at URL: www.unison-scotland.org.uk/briefings/directpay.html (accessed May 2006)

Williams, V. and Holman, A. (2006) 'Direct payments and autonomy: issues for people with learning difficulties', in Leece, J. and Bornat, J. (eds) (2006) *Developments in Direct Payments,* Bristol: Policy Press

Witcher, S., Stalker, K., Roadburg, M. and Jones, C. (2000) *Direct Payments: The Impact on Choice and Control for Disabled People,* Edinburgh: Scottish Executive, Central Research Unit

Wood, R. (1991) 'Care of disabled people', in Dalley, G. (ed) (1991) *Disability and Social Policy,* London: Policy Studies Institute

Zarb, G. and Nadash, P. (1994) *Cashing in on Independence: Comparing the Costs and Benefits of Cash and Services,* London: BCODP.

Index